Computing Organizational Behavior

Computing Organizational Behavior

Anupama Sakhare

PARTRIDGE

Copyright © 2018 by Anupama Sakhare.

ISBN: Hardcover   978-1-5437-0265-1
         Softcover   978-1-5437-0264-4
         eBook   978-1-5437-0271-2

All rights reserved. No part of this book may be used or reproduced by any means, graphic, electronic, or mechanical, including photocopying, recording, taping or by any information storage retrieval system without the written permission of the author except in the case of brief quotations embodied in critical articles and reviews.

Because of the dynamic nature of the Internet, any web addresses or links contained in this book may have changed since publication and may no longer be valid. The views expressed in this work are solely those of the author and do not necessarily reflect the views of the publisher, and the publisher hereby disclaims any responsibility for them.

Print information available on the last page.

To order additional copies of this book, contact
Partridge India
000 800 10062 62
orders.india@partridgepublishing.com

www.partridgepublishing.com/india

CONTENTS

	PREFACE	xi
1.	**INTRODUCTION**	1
1.1	Organizational Structure	2
1.2	Factors Criticaly Affecting Employee Productivity	3
1.3	Existing Enterprise Resource Planning Approach	5
1.4	The Existing Scenario	6
1.5	Problem Definition For Computerized Confidential Report Processing	6
1.6	Research Objective	6
1.7	Scope of Work	13
1.8	Decision-Oriented Model	14
1.9	Behavior Computing Model With Experimental Design	15
1.10	Advantages Of The Model	16
1.11	Product Utility	17
1.12	Process With Rule - Base	18
1.13	Methodology Proposed For Behavior Computing	22
1.14	Cluster Analysis	36
1.15	Computational Processing Steps	38
2.	**DATA PROCESSING OF CATEGORY A EMPLOYEES**	47
2.1	Method-1: 'euclidean' and 'average'	47
2.2	Method-2: 'euclidean' and 'centroid'	48
2.3	Method-3: 'euclidean' and 'complete'	49
2.4	Method-4: 'euclidean' and 'median'	50

2.5	Method-5: Euclidean and Single	51
2.6	Method-6: Euclidean and Ward	52
2.7	Method-7: Euclidean and weighted	53
2.8	Method-8: Chebychev and average	54
2.9	Method-9: Mahalanobis and average	55
2.10	Method-10: Cosine and average	56
2.11	Method-11: Cityblock and average	57
2.12	Method-12: Seuclidean and single	58
2.13	Method-13: cityblock and single	59
2.14	Method-14: Hamming and average	60
2.15	Method-15: Jaccard and average	61
2.16	Method-16: seuclidean and centroid	62
2.17	Method-17: cityblock and centroid	63
2.18	Method-18: Minkowski and centroid	64
2.19	Method-19: chebychev and centroid	65
2.20	Method-20: Mahalanobis and centroid	66
2.21	Method-21: Cosine and centroid	67
2.22	Method-22: Minkowski and single	68
2.23	Method-23: Mahalanobis and single	69
2.24	Method-24: Hamming and Centroid	70
2.25	Method-25: Jaccard and centroid	71
2.26	Method-26: Seuclidean and complete	72
2.27	Method-27: cityblock and complete	73
2.28	Method-28: Minkowski and complete	74
2.29	Method-29: chebychev and complete	75
2.30	Method-30: Mahalanobis and Complete	76
3.	**DATA PROCESSING OF CATEGORY B EMPLOYEES**	79
3.1	Method-1: 'euclidean' and 'average'	79
3.2	Method-2: 'euclidean' and 'centroid'	80
3.3	Method-3: 'euclidean' and 'median'	81
3.4	Method-4: 'euclidean' and 'ward'	82

3.5	Method-5: 'seuclidean' and 'average'	83
3.6	Method-6: 'cityblock' and 'average'	84
3.7	Method-7: 'minkowski' and 'average'	85
3.8	Method-8: chebychev and average	86
3.9	Method-9: Mahalanobis and average	87
3.10	Method-10: Cosine and average	88
3.11	Method-11: Cosine and complete	89
3.12	Method-12: correlation and average	90
3.13	Method-13: Spearman and average	91
3.14	Method-14: Hamming and average	92
3.15	Method-15: Jaccard and average	93
3.16	Method-16: Seuclidean and centroid	94
3.17	Method-17: Cityblock and centroid	95
3.18	Method-18: Minkowski and centroid	96
3.19	Method-19: Chebychew and centroid	97
3.20	Method-20: Mahalanobis and centroid	98
3.21	Method-21: Cosine and centroid	99
3.22	Method-22:Correlation and centroid	100
3.23	Method-23: Spearman and centroid	101
3.24	Method-24: Hamming and centroid	102
3.25	Method-25 Jaccard and centroid	103
3.26	Method-26: Euclidean and complete	104
3.27	Method-27: Seuclidean and complete	105
3.28	Method- 28: Cityblock and complete	106
3.29	Method-29: Minkowski and complete	107
3.30	Method-30: Chebychev and complete	108
4.	**DATA PROCESSING OF CATEGORY C EMPLOYEES**	111
4.1	Method-1: 'euclidean' and 'average'	111
4.2	Method-2: 'euclidean' and 'centroid'	112
4.3	Method-3: 'euclidean' and 'complete'	113
4.4	Method-4: 'euclidean' and 'median'	114

4.5	Method-5: Euclidean and Single	115
4.6	Method-6: Euclidean and Ward	116
4.7	Method-7: Euclidean and weighted	117
4.8	Method-8: Chebychev and average	118
4.9	Method-9: Mahalanobis and average	119
4.10	Method-10: Cosine and average	120
4.11	Method-11: Citiyblock and average	121
4.12	Method-12: Seuclidean and single	122
4.13	Method-13: cityblock and single	123
4.14	Method-14: Hamming and average	124
4.15	Method-15: Jaccard and average	125
4.16	Method-16: seuclidean and centroid	126
4.17	Method-17: cityblock and centroid	127
4.18	Method-18: Minkowski and centroid	128
4.19	Method-19: chebychev and centroid	129
4.20	Method-20: Mahalanobis and centroid	130
4.21	Method-21: Cosine and centroid	131
4.22	Method-22: Minkowski and single	132
4.23	Method-23: Mahalanobis and single	133
4.24	Method-24: Hamming and Centroid	134
4.25	Method-25: Jaccard and centroid	135
4.26	Method-26: Seuclidean and complete	136
4.27	Method-27: cityblock and complete	137
4.28	Method- 28: Minkowski and complete	138
4.29	Method-29: chebychev and complete	139
4.30	Method-30: Mahalanobis and Complete	140
5.	**FOR CATEGORY-D EMPLOYEES**	143
5.1	Method-1: euclidean and single	143
5.2	Method-2: euclidean and complete	144
5.3	Method-3: euclidean & average	145
5.4	Method-4: euclidean and centroid	146

5.5	Method-5: Seuclidean and single	147
5.6	Method-6: Seuclidean and complete	148
5.7	Method-7: Seulidean and average	149
5.8	Method-8: Seluclidean and centroid	150
5.9	Method-9: Cityblock and single	151
5.10	Method-10: Cityblock and complete	152
5.11	Method-11: Cityblock and average	153
5.12	Method-12: Cityblock and centroid	154
5.13	Method-13: Minkowski and single	155
5.14	Method-14: Minkowski and complete	156
5.15	Method-15: Minkowski and average	157
5.16	Method-16: Minkowski and centroid	158
5.17	Method-17: Chebychev and single	159
5.18	Method-18: Chebychev and complete	160
5.19	Method-19: Chebychev and average	161
5.20	Method-20: Chebychev and centroid	162
5.21	Method-21: Mahalanobis and single	163
5.22	Method-22: Mahalanobis and complete	164
5.23	Method-23: Mahalanobis and average	165
5.24	Method-24: Mahalanobis and centroid	166
5.25	Method-25: Cosine and single	167
5.26	Method-26: Cosine and complete	168
5.27	Method-27: Cosine and average	169
5.28	Method-28: Cosine and centroid	170
5.29	Method-29: Correlation and single	171
5.30	Method-30: Correlation and complete	172
5.31	Method-31: Correlation and average	173
5.32	Method-32: Correlation and centroid	174
5.33	Method-33: Spearman and single	175
5.34	Method-34: Spearman and complete	176
5.35	Method-35: Spearman and average	177

5.36	Method-36: Spearman and centroid	178
5.37	Method-37: Hamming and single	179
5.38	Method-38: Hamming and complete	180
5.39	Method-39: Hamming and average	181
5.40	Method-40: Hamming and centroid	182
5.41	Method-41: Jaccard and single	183
5.42	Method-42: Jaccard and complete	184
5.43	Method-43: Jaccard and average	185
5.44	Method-44: Jaccard and centroid	186

PREFACE

The present work relates to the Experimental Study of Natural Behavior Computing Paradigms A new model of Enterprise Computing based on Human-Resource and its management is developed using the concept of Employee-Behaviour Computing and is experimentally studied and presented in this work.

The conceptual extracts of Nature and its functional processes are borrowed to create new mathematical models in truly mimicked form to develop Computational Paradigms called Natural Behavior Computing Paradigms.

None of the existing Enterprise Resource Planning Modules related to H-R field discuss about methods to solve the problem of personnel productivity and to investigate why do employee teams fail to unit and gel together and what are the existing causes which create problems related to the Attitude of an individual Employee when he or she is working for an organization. The motive of an employees working in the University Organization is actually based on the Intrinsic and extrinsic objectives set by one single individual employee.

The unit of Human Resource and Development rests upon the foundations laid down at the University level. The present work offers computational methods for finding good quality people as employees into jobs so that they do well in terms of Integrity and achieve higher Productivity. It is therefore important to investigate the relationship of the Productivity of the employee measured using a test of Activity based on the General Intelligence of the employee and the Natural Behavioural Attributes which relate to the Behavioural Integrity of an employee.

In the present work a study of the Comparative Performance of individual employees is conducted by using the Scores of their: (i) General Intelligence (GI) and (ii) Behavioural Integrity (BI) by using the Synthetic Data of Grade-A,B.C and D employees working in a University.

Human Resources and Personnel Planning Development is a module in the Enterprise Resource Management system which is concerned with the self development of employees. The purpose of personnel planning is to determine who will be required and when to perform a particular task specially to avoid violence and organizational rivalry at work.

The personal Organizational Behaviour attributes of an employee are based on various Quality factors such as morality-attribute, truthfulness- attribute, generosity-attribute, determination-attribute, renunciation- attribute, patience- attribute, wisdom-attribute, effort- attribute, equanimity-attribute and the loving-kindness attribute. All these attributes are inter-related to each other and project the success or failure of an Organization.

In the present work the Morality attribute is used to compute a new Human-Resource module to investigate Natural Clusters of employees to explore Employee-Behaviour Computing in the University Organization.

The Data Mining Software is used to find the measurement of correlation if it exits between the two sets of Behavioural Integrity Score and the General Intelligence Score.

A two-tailed test is used to perform Hypothesis Testing worked on the data of 100 Employees of the University Organization by using Synthetic data of randomly selected 25 employees from each Category – A,B,C and D Category and at a significance level of .05 we find that the values of The Data Mining Cluster Procedures are used to find the correlation for each category.

Anupama Sakhare

INTRODUCTION

CHAPTER - I

CHAPTER 1

INTRODUCTION

1.1 Introduction

Natural Behavior Computing is an area concerned with the intelligence acquired from the Natural phenomena. Natural Clusters are those groups which are having a common attribute for forming collectivism. Examples of natural clusters include flock of birds, fish school, rock textures, beautforce velocities and era of evolution to name a few. Employee Clusters are natural clusters of employees found in an Organization which are formed on the basis of their individual and group Organizational Behaviour.

In the present Higher Education University Scenario it is observed that there are various problems existing in the country. Due to such problems our youth and employed personnel are found to resign their jobs and joint other Enterprises. But even then the problem exists. In short there is a "Brain - Drain". This Lacuna is due to the Higher Educational system and due to other causes such as:

(1) Problems with Data Governance
(2) Problems with Integrity
(3) Problems related to social and culture gaps such as Gender, Color, Skin – types, Caste, Religion, Linguistic Patterns, Regional Disjoints and Barriers created.

As a result the employees working in the University organization have come up with some easy solutions such as fake degree printing, manipulations in the marksheet, Barter system of exchange to provide degrees. Exploitation of Girls and Women at work, Sexual Harrasment subsequently giving rise to crime in the country.

1.1 Organizational Structure

The Rashtrasant Tukodoji Maharaj Nagpur University was established in the year 1923, which is one of oldest set up university of Central India.

The RTM Nagpur University has the following organizational structure

1. The senate
2. The management council
3. The Academic faculty
4. Board of colleges and university development
5. Board of studies.
6. Board of Inter Disciplinary studies
7. Board of Examinations.
8. Board of Adult and continuing Education and Extension Services
9. The students council
10. Board of University Teaching and Research.
11. Bodies designated by statutes.

There are 40 Educational Departments. The Employee Organization is categorized into the following types:

Category 'A'
Category 'B'
Category 'C'
Category 'D' employees.

For the development of the proposed system a survey was conducted by the author to find and explore the status of Employment in the University Organization.

1.2 Factors Criticaly Affecting Employee Productivity

The performance of an individual employee in an organization and the job satisfaction achieved by the employee depends on different factors which ultimately affect the productivity of an employee. These important factors were identified by Hofstead which are defined as value dimensions. During late 1970s a research was conducted by Geerrt Hofstede to identify International values which vary with National Culture.

Cultural Values:

The Cultural values are the care and fundamental values which are possessed by all individuals at the National Level and are accepted by all the people working throughout a particular organization. They are defined as six dimensions of culture. These six dimensions are accepted by researchers and managers worldwide. They are: (1) Power distance, (2), individualism vs. Collectivism (3) Masculinity vs. Feminity (4) Uncertainty Avoidance. (5) Long – term vs. short – term orientation and (6) Indulgence vs. restraint.

A score – Matrix was generated to find the score of a country with respect to the six – dimensions. The score was in the range of 1 meaning extremely low and a particular dimension to 100 for extremely high.

Hofstede's Matrix projects the following scenario about Indian Organizations.

(1) Country India Power Distance : 77
(2) Individualism versus Collaborative Working : 48

(3) Masculinity versus Feminity : 50
(4) Uncertainty Avoidance : 40
(5) Orientation : 51
(6) Indulgence versus Restraint : 26

Power Distance is Unequal distribution of power in the organization. Individualism is the degree or extent upto which people prefer to work individually rather than as a group.

Masculinity is the national cultural attribute where the male and female roles are defined. Male is considered as the karta of the family or the Organization. Feminity indicates that there is a very little difference between male and female roles in the organization.

Orientation attribute both long-term and short-term orientation is a national – culture Attribute which mean respect for tradition and the fulfillment of social laws and obligations.

Indulgence versus Restraint is the attribute by which the social conduct of an employee is evaluated whether the person enjoys life, performs sexual misconduct in the organization or outside. It determines the quality and extent of an individual to enjoy life, have fun and fulfil his/her Natural Human Desires in the organization.

From the score-Matrix based on International values versus six Dimensions we are concerned more about the two factors:

Power Distance & : 77%
Restraint : 26%

For Power Distance attribute 77% which includes the misconduct such as killing, Theft and False speech for which the employee is responsible. It is found that power is not distributed equally in the organization and the behavior of the people in the context of Restraint is very less and maximum number of people are involved in indulgence such as consumption of intoxicating drinks, drugs and enjoy life by sexual misconduct.

These two factors are very important because they are responsible for breaking five precepts. The five precept are given by Rashtrasant Tukadoji Maharaj.

The HR-Module manages the Human Resources and its applications and it provides an integrated solution as a HR – Management system by using two subsystems. These subsystems are:

HR – PD and
HR – PA

Components of HR – Module:

In the existing enterprise Resource Planning Systems the HR-PD is concerned with the Personnel – Planning and Development system and HR-PA is about the Personnel Administration.

1.3 Existing Enterprise Resource Planning Approach:

In the existing HR-Module related to Personnel Development presently the approach used assumes that the organization has recruited good people who will continue to stay in the organization and they will be provided with opportunities and the required knowledge and skills so that their performance and productivity would improve.

But inspite of the desired qualifications, skills and the opportunities offered by the organization the potential of the employees in terms of productivity is lacking due to Human –factors.

1.4 The Existing Scenario:

The newness about the present model developed is to provide additional functionality to the Human Resource Module.

In the traditional existing Organizational structure it is observed that the performance of an individual employee is judged using the Appraisal Reports and the Confidential Report.

The Appraisal Reports have three components which relate to:

(1) Training provided
(2) Research and Development and
(3) Extension Activities performed by an individual employee.

The Confidential Report has two major components which relate to:

Academic / Job-oriented Achievements
Abilities related to conduct.

The Confidential Report (CR) is collected annually by the senior officials in the organization as an input to the Decision Support System at the management level but it is a futile practice and effort.

1.5 Problem Definition For Computerized Confidential Report Processing:

To determine if there exists a correlation between Behavioural Integrity and General Intelligence.

1.6 Research Objective

1. To study the basic Natural Behavior Computing Paradigms specifically related to Natural Clusters.

2. To develop models to measure Employee Productivity using General Clustering Criteria.

The research objectives are as follows:

In the study a model is prepared which relates to the Human Resource Module of Enterprise Resource Planning. The model is used to measure Employee Productivity and it is used to find the mutual relationship between two important variables studied in the Organization Behaviour domain. These two variables are the Behavioral Integrity of the an employee and the General Intelligence of the employee. Clustering methods are used to evaluate the cluster linkages in the study: (1) single, (2) complete (3) average and (4) centroid methods. A hypothesis is framed to check if the Behavioral Integrity is positively correlated to the General Intelligence of an Employee.

The measurement of Employee productivity in the University Organization is judged by the attribute called General Intelligence.

General ability which is also called general Intelligence is the ability of an individual employee to reason and it is considered to be involved in all the activities and the intellectual abilities performed by the employee as an individual.

There are 2 important factors which are used to Test the General Intelligence (GI) which includes:-

(1) Test of speed
(2) Perfection of work which taken together decide the actual productivity of an Employee.

The Estimate of general ability and character of Employees working in the organization is reviewed and reported to a senior officer aa a grading Assessment.

This data regarding as the following parameters:

(1) Behavioral Integrity (BI) and (2) General Intelligence (GI) which is collected by using an Annual Confidential Report.

A claims statement is uses to create an initial hypothesis statement in the following form which is reframed from the claim statement

H_0 = Behavioral Integrity (BI) is not related to General Intelligence (GI).
H_A: BI is positively related to (GI)

The objectives of the experimental study include the following:

1. To study the basics of Natural Clusters using the known Natural Computing Techniques.
2. To study different test problems related to Cluster Experiments
3. To gain insight into the four General Clustering Paradigms. These paradigms are

3.1 Single Linkage
3.2 Complete Linkage
3.3 Average Linkage
3.4 Centroid Linkage

Measurment of Employee Productivity- First Criteria:

The BI – Score Matrix is created Next the GI score Matrix is created. A combined Matrix (2 Dimensional Matrix) is created which holds BI and GI score of 25 Employees. Four matrices are created for category – A, category – B, category-C and category – D Employees.

The estimation is done using the performance Score Rating using the following ordinal scale.

Sr.No.	GI Score	Remark	Grade	Numeric Score Value
1	>= 85	Outstanding	A	5
2	85-70	Very good	B	4
3	69-60	Good	C	3
4	61-40	Average	D	2
5	<40	Below Average	E	1

This numeric value viz. (5,4,3,2,1) are stored as the GI- Score.

The Behavioral Integrity (BI) is computed for every employee using precept Rule – Base.

Sr.No.	Precept	Presence - Absence
1	P1	0/1
2	P2	0/1
3	P3	0/1
4	P4	0/1
5	P5	0/1

Where

P1: Abstinence from killing
P2: Abstinence from taking what is not given
P3: Abstinence from sexual Misconduct
P4: Abstinence from false speech
P5: Abstinence from consuming intoxicating drinks and drugs.

Performing Cluster Experiments

Data Mining Software is used to perform cluster Experiments. Cluster Analysis for the determination of Natural Clusters is done using Hierarchical Clustering Algorithms.

These Algorithms are:

(1) Single Linkage
(2) Average Linkage
(3) Complete Linkage
(4) Centroid Linkage

The following methods are used to compute Pairwise distance:

(1) Euclidean (2) Seuclidean, (3) Cityblock, (4) Minkewski (5) Chebychev (6) Mahalanobis (7) Cosine (8) Correlation (9) Spearman (10) Hamming (11) Jaccard.

Computational steps:

Step 1: A two dimensional 2x25 matrix is generated with two values of BI and GI for 25- Individual Employees of Category – A.
Step 2: Pairwise distance is computed.
P-dist is computed
Step 3:
Square form is generated
Step 4:
Cluster Linkage is computed
Step 5:
Cophenetic Correlation co-efficient is computed.
Step 6:
Inconsistency co-efficient schedule is generated.
Step 7:
Four General Clustering Criteria Models are used to prepare the Aggmerative Schedule.
Step 8:
The four models are compared using the values of cophenetic correlation Co-efficient and Dendrogram is generated.

Similarly the above mentioned eight steps are repeated for other employee categories and 3 such similar cluster Experiments are conducted for: (1) Category – B, (2) Category - C and (3) Category – D Employees.

Conducting Data Analytics

(1) The inter connectedness amongst the employees is evaluated
(2) Dissimilarity amongst the employees is evaluated.
(3) Dendrogram is used to visualize the Hierarchical Cluster Linkages.
(4) The value of cophenetic correlation co-efficient is evaluated for all the four models. If the value of cophenetic correlation co-efficient is greater than 0.6 then it is interpreted that the variable BI and GI are positively correlated.

Phase Assessment of Experimental Claims:

The question which arises at this phase is how do we make a correct assessment of the Experimental Claims made in the Experimental Study. And other questions such as:

(1) Is the model valid?
(2) Is the model developed Reliable?
(3) Is the model developed Generalizable?
(4) Are the statements in the Hypothesis precise?

The author has observed positive responses for all these four questions.

The reasoning is performed with Statistical Analysis.

A tentative statement of hypothesis which says that "BI is not related to GI" as null hypothesis and it is accompanied by an Alternative Hypothesis which states "BI is positively related to GI"

Evaluation conducted in the present paradigm:

The present model employs Cluster Experimental Designs. The evaluation conducted in this paradigm has the following components:

[1] [1] Inputs
[2] [2] Process
[3] [3] Outputs

[1] Inputs: There are two inputs based on the employee characteristics. BI is the independent variable and GI is the dependent variable.

[2] Process: Statistical Analysis is performed to evaluate. The Hypothesis. Field Experiment was conducted to find the scores of Behavioral Integrity and General Intelligence by using the Confidential Report - generated values of BI and GI.

The cause and effect relationship is computed. This is implied by the statement made in the hypothesis.

The strength of this cause and effect relationship which exists between behavioral Integrity and general Intelligence of an employee is computed by using a function called cophenetic correlation co-efficient.

The unit of 100 employees is divided into 4 groups with 25 employees from category – A, B, C and D respectively

The following tests are performed:

[1] t – Distribution test (for 25 Employees)
[2] 2 way - ANOVA
[3] F – Test
[4] Cophenetic Correlation Co-efficient
[5] Spearman's Rank correlation co-efficient.

1.7 Scope of Work

The scope of the research work is related to the Hypothetical University – Organization Case which has both Teaching and Non-Teaching Employees working together.

Population:

Only 100 – Employees of the University are considered for the study. The total population of 100 Employees is split into the following types:-

1) Sample – 1: Category - A - 25 Employees
2) Sample – 2: Category – B - 25 Employees
3) Sample – 3: Category – C – 25 Employees
4) Sample – 4: Category – D - 25 Employees

Data:

The data used for the model is of type – synthetic Data. Synthetic Data is used in the project to preserve confidentiality. Since both the input variables – Behavioral Integrity and General intelligence are derived from the Confidential Report of the Employee.

3. Distribution:

The data collected is of ordinal type initially but then it is converted in Discrete Type (0/1). The score Matrix is generated for 25-Employees which stores the BI and GI scores.

Four Cluster Experiments are Conducted in the study for:

(1) Category - A
(2) Category – B
(3) Category – C
(4) Category – D

The values of BI and GI are in the range of (1 to 5) which do not vary to a large extent therefore instead of Standard Normal Distribution, pure Normal Distribution is used in the study.

Linkage Metric Selection for comparison:

For the present study out of the known 7 methods only 4 methods are choosen for the study, that is, single, complete, average and centroid cluster linkages.

Population: 100 employees of four employee category are randomly chosen.

Sample size: 25 (25x4)

Distribution: Normal Distribution N (0,1) with unit Normal Distribution Significance Level: The Significance Level (alpha = 0.05)

1.8 Decision-Oriented Model:

MAJOR CHARACTERISTICS OF THE PROPOSED ORGANIZATIONAL BEHAVIOR BASED DECISION - ORIENTED MODEL:

In the present project a new model is proposed for the H-R module of Enterprise Resource Computing Environment.

This computed model is based on the practical application of the precepts Theory found in the values discipline of Organizational behavior. The precept Rue base considered in this project is based on Rashtrasant Tukadoji Maharaj's Philosophical Thoughts authored in his book "Gram Geeta".

This model has following characteristics:

(1) Clear problem statement with well stated goals.
(2) For achieving the goal a precept Rule – Base is created using the CR – of employees.
(3) Work - Productivity is checked using the two important criteria:
    (i) Time Required to complete a task.
    (ii) Whether the task is done completely and perfectly.
(4) A causal hypothesis is established to find whether there is essentially any relationship between Behavioural Integrity and the General Intelligence of an individual employee.
(5) This model has a long-term goal and perspective. Since it can be applied to any other organization and useful in Enterprise Resource Planning.
(6) This model is assumed to be stable for Restructuring Organizational Structure.
(7) This model is useful for Decision Makers which can be brilliantly used for work Team Creation.
(8) This model would enhance the Administrative Ability and work as a decision – support model for flexible integrated Manpower Planning System.

1.9 Behavior Computing Model With Experimental Design:

This modle makes use of Experimental Design. The experimental design approach makes use of the following phases. These phases are:

[i]   Phase 1: Sampling Phase
[ii] Phase 2: Establishing a claim statement
[iii] Phase 3: Setting up Objectives

[iv] Phase 4: Measuring Employee Productivity
[v] Phase 5: Cluster Experiment
[vi] Phase 6: Conducting Data Analytics
[vii] Phase 7: Assessment of the Experimental claims
[viii] Phase 8: Reasoning with Statistical Analysis computational-Tools are used to develop this model.

Data Details:

Cluster sampling is applied to Natural Cluster of Employees. The present study is conducted on a total population of 100 University Employees and Synthetic Data is used in the study.

The population of 100 Employees includes a Randomly choosen set of 25 Employees belonging to the following categories:

(1) (1) Category – 'A' Employee
(2) (2) Category – 'B' Employee
(3) (3) Category – 'C' Employee
(4) (4) Category – 'D' Employee

1.10 Advantages Of The Model:

The model generated has the following advantages:

(1) Its time complexity is $O(kn^2)$ which is less compared to the existing models.
(2) The space complexity is very less and it amounts to $O(n^2)$.
(3) The model makes use of very simple Hierarchical Computational Techniques.
(4) The model uses parametric methods which are easily computable.
(5) Affinity Matrix can be easily constructed using this model.
(6) Time – series Analysis can be computed by adding time component in the score – Matrix.

(7) Trend Analysis over a period of time can be generated to examine the changing trend.
(8) Pattern mining related to a particular Organization can be performed using this model.
(9) The properties of the existing social Networks Cluster which exhibit the known Evolutionary Characteristics can be found and the following Natural Laws can be examined on the basis of cause and effect relationships. Densification Power - Law and
Shrinking – Diameter Law can be easily evaluated using this model.
(10) The Application of this model can be made to design a Recommender System, Human – Resource Intelligence System and Knowledge – Tone Application can be created for decision support system.

DISADVANTAGES OF THE MODEL:

(1) The high dimensionality of population posses problems.
(2) It is difficult and challenging to design a model with organizational behavior functionality.
(3) The variance between the input variables may be large and it is difficult to measure the similarlity.
(4) The selection of the clustering method and the number of clusters to be choosen may pose difficult problems.
(5) This model does not specify how to deal with Tie – situation
(6) Variance – Inflation factors create problems with respet to multicollinearity which yields incoherent - outputs.
(7) Variability of data and skewness in Data Distribution cannot be handled by this model.

1.11 Product Utility:

The proposed product is a software module developed for a public organization and pertains to Human Resource Development.

At the National Level the Ministry of Human Resource Development Department looks after the need of the country's Human Resource at the Standard of Higher Education with the University Organizations.

The basic objectives of Universities in the Country are to:

Provide Higher Education
To promote girls in the field of Education
To support Research and Development
To offer Employment Opportunities to Youth and Old.
To provide a secular and conducive Environment to the Educated and people without formal Education.

1.12 Process With Rule - Base:

Cluster analysis is used to perform the natural divisions in data. In order to test the hypothesis initially cophenetic co-relations coefficient is used. The productivity of an employee is measured in two contexts:

Behavioral Integrity and
General Intelligence

RULE – BASE:

Two Rule - Bases are used to evaluate:

The GI measurement and
The BI measurement

Operational Rules for GI:

Rule 1: Work Completion Time
Rule 2: Perfection of work

A Rule – base is used to find the measurement of GI using the following table.

Table 1 GI Score

S.No.	GI Score	GI Grade	Measure Numeric Value
1	>= 85 Outstanding	A	5
2	84-70 Very Good	B	4
3	69-61 Good	C	3
4	60-40 Average	D	2
5	< 40 Below Average	E	1

Operational Rules for BI:

The BI score is obtained by using the precept–score which is compared using the precept –Rule – base. The precept score is based on the rule –base by using the employee's Natural precept attributes based on his/her behavioral habits.

Table 2: Rule – Base for BI

S.No.	Precept	Absence - 0 Presence – 1
1	P1: Abstinence from killing	0/1
2	P2: Abstinence from taking which is not given	0/1
3	P3: Abstinence from sexual misconduct	0/1
4	P4: Abstinence from false speech	0/1
5	P5: Abstinence from intoxicating drinks and drugs	0/1

By using the precept measurements a Behavioral – Integrity (BI) score Matrix is generated.

Table 3: BI Score Matrix

Employee	P1	P2	P3	P4	P5	Total score
E1	1	1	1	1	1	5
E2	1	0	1	1	0	3
E3	1	1	0	0	0	2
E4	1	1	1	1	0	4
E5	0	1	1	0	0	2

Data Mining Software is used to define the two dimensional covariance matrix. The computational processing is performed using the following steps:

Step 1: A score matrix is created for 25 – Employees of a particular category.

Step 2: The pair-wise distance is computed for individual employee.

Step 3: The squareform is generated.

Step 4: Cluster Linkage is computed

Step 5: The co-phenetic correlation co-efficient is computed.

Step 6: The Inconsistency co-efficient is computed.

Step 7: The Natural Divisions in Data are evaluated.

Step 8: The Dendrogram is generated.

The next phase of the study is to perform Data Analysis During this phase the Co-phenetic co-rrelation co-efficient is computed for category – A, Category – B, Category – C and Category – D by using four cluster linkages viz. Single, complete, average and centroid methods.

The data flow of the proposed system is presented in the form of a Context Analysis Diagram shown below.

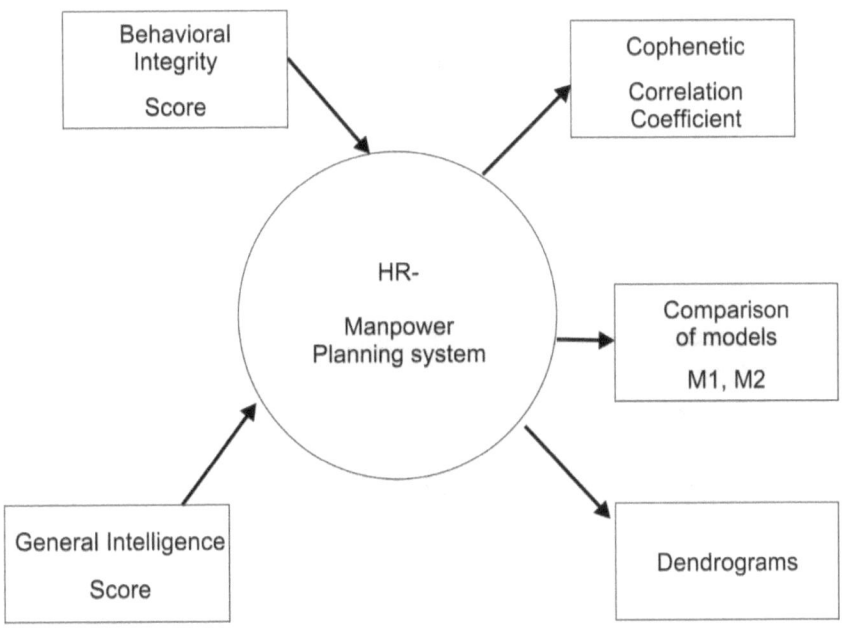

Fig. 1 : Context Analysis Diagram

Fig. 1 Shows the Context Analysis Diagram with the input entities- BI-score Matrix and GI – Score Matrix.

There is a Single process in the Context Analysis Diagram which shows the HR – Manpower Planning System which is used to find the mutual relationship of the two variables – Behavioral Integrity and General Intelligence.

1.13 Methodology Proposed For Behavior Computing:

Within a known population, there are different groups which are similar to each other in some way although the internal groups found within the population have a wide variety of variations in the internal domain. Such groups are called Natural Clusters and sampling method are used in natural clusters. Natural Cluster sampling which is used to study the total population of 100 employees choosen randomly. Consist of the set of 100 which is divided into 4 – parts related to the teaching and Non-Teaching Employees of the University. Twenty five (25) employees of each category are choosen randomly. These are

(1) Category - 'A' Employee
(2) Category - 'B' Employee
(3) Category - 'C' Employee
(4) Category - 'D' Employee

The following cluster Linkage Algorithms are used: (1) Single (2) Complete (3) Average and (4) Centroid.

These four models are compared for a population of 100 employees.

Inputs:

The following two matrices are used to create the 4 models.

(1) BI Matrix and
(2) GI Matrix

BI Matrix is used to store the behavioral integrity score of each employee.

GI Matrix is used to store the General Intelligence score of the employee.

The Hypothesis Testing can be performed reasonably well because the entire population of 100 employees is evaluated for finding the employee productivity.

Cluster Analysis is used to perform the natural divisions in data. The Hypothesis is framed to check if there a positive correlation between Behavioral Integrity (BI) and general Intelligence (GI) of Employees.

Hopkins statistics is used to find whether the statistics is Homogenous or Non-homogenous.

Hierarchical Clustering Algorithms are used in the study which do not depend on any priori label but on the Adjacency Matrix created using Cluster Linkage Algorithms.

Outputs: The following statistical Tools are used to perform Hypothesis Testing

The following tests are performed:-

Test 1: t – Test: If h = 1 then alternative

Test 2: F – Test: large value of F leads to rejection of the Null hypothesis.

Test 3: ANOVA
2- way ANOVA is used to find the Analysis of variance when the data is classified on the basis of two factors

Test 4: P-value test
The value of $p \approx 0.0000$ relates to the acceptance of H_A and rejection of H_o.

Test: 5:
Standard error of the estimate: This is denoted by S. Smaller values of S are preferred.

Test 6:
If the computed value of cophenetic correlation coefficient is greater 0.6 then the variables are positively correlated.

Test 7:
If the value of spearman's Rank correlation is close to 1 then the null hypothesis is rejected. Spearman's Rank correlation is evaluated as follows:

X = []; y = pdist (X)
Z = Linkage (Y, 'average")
[C,D] = cophenet (Z, Y)
r = corr (Y,D, 'type', 'spearman')

Two Sample tt - test

The function tt test 2 () is used to determine the two-sample tt –test sample 1: Category – A Sample 2: Category B.

The following format is used:
hh = tt test 2 (x,y, alpha, tail)

COMPARATIVE STUDY OF THE TWO MODELS:
Two models are compared in this study.

xx = [0.7126, 0.6701, 0.7075, 0.7075]
xy = [0.7810, 0.7074, 0.8087, 0.8085]

Significance level:
The default value, of x = 0.05 the option 'both' is specified for Two-tailed tests since $\mu \neq \mu_0$ as specified in the Hypothesis

H= tt test 2 (x,y)
hh = 1
hh = tt test 2 (x,y, 0.05, 'both')

Output: The output of the test is returned in hh. If hh=1 indicates a rejection of the null hypothesis at the default significance level

Alpha = 0.05

If hh = 0 it indicates a failure to reject thenull hypothesis at the 5% significance level. Thus, H_A is accepted i.e. BI is positively related to GI

Since the sample size is < 30 t – distribution statistics is applied. Two sample t-test is performed on the following matrix.

Model	Sample-1	Sample-2	Sample-3	Sample-4
1	0.7126	0.6701	0.7075	0.7075
2	0.7810	0.7074	0.8087	0.8085

Two models are evaluated

Size of sample – 1: 25 – employees of category A.

Size of Sample 2: 25 – Employees of category B.

Size of Sample 3: 25 – Employees of category C.

Size of Sample 4: 25 – Employees of category D.

Model -1: pertains to 'single' Hierarchical Linkage

Model -2: Pertains to 'complete' Hierarchical Linkage

The values of cophenetic correlation coefficient of model – 1 are stored in Matrix X.

The values of cophenetic correlation coefficient of model-2 are stored in Matrix Y.

HYPOTHESIS TESTING USING CRITICAL VALUES:

Test – t Test – type: Two tailed. For N (0,1) – Distribution Hypothesis Testing for Mean

Confidence Level	Confidence Co-efficient	α	Critical value
95%	0.95	0.05	2.731

Conditions for t – Distribution:
   (i) Distribution - Normal
   (ii) Variances are equal
   (iii) Level of significance for two-tailed test = 0.05
   (iv) Degrees of freedom (d.f) = 5

The critical values for t – distribution with 15 d.f are - 2.731 and + 2.731.

If the computed value of t-Test statistics falls outside the range (-2.731 and +2.731) we reject null hypothesis, H_0.

Critical values for
Two – way ANOVA:

(In an experimental design without repeated values)

The ANOVA Table is used to test the Hypothesis

If the between – sample variance is large when all the effects of the observed treatments are different.

   (1) F – Distribution at α = 0.05 If the computed value of F is large we reject the null Hypothesis. Computed value of F is larger than the Table value.
   (2) Significance F: P – Value Approach for Hypothesis Testing. P – Value(s)

The values of probability > F value are used to test the hypothesis

If $p \approx 0.0000$, then the null hypothesis is rejected.

If we observe that p-values (Significance F) in ANOVA table are

0.0011
0.0138
are much smaller than 0.05, then the null hypothesis is rejected.

Analysis of Variance:

2-way ANOVA is used for Hypothesis Testing

Step 1: The population with equal means is choosen
Step 2: The following values are evaluated

1. The between column variance
2. The within column variance
3. Ratio of F.

Step 3: ANOVA table is generated. It has five columns. The first column shows the source of the variability.

The second column shows the sum of squares (ss) due to each source.

The third shows the degree of freedom (df) associated with each source.

The fourth shows the mean squares (Ms) which is the ratio ss/df

The fifth column shows the F-statistics which is the ratio of the mean squares.

Load model – matrix
P= anova 2 (model – matrix)

Example ANOVA Table

Source	SS	Df	MS	F	Prob > F
Columns	0.04433	3	0.01478	13.48	0.0011
Rows	0.2064	3	0.00688	6.28	0.0138
Error	0.00986	9	0.0011		
Total	0.7483	15			

If $p \approx 0.0000$, the null hypothesis is rejected.

Another variation of the syntax is as follows:

P – anova 2 (X, reps, display opt)

Where, reps is the number replicates in each position

The display (opt is 'on' by default and it is used to display the ANOVA Table.

Hypothesis Testing
Paradigm I:

1. Claim: The Existing Training Programme does not influence the Productivity
2. Null Hypothesis (Ho): $\mu = \mu$
   Blscore Glscore
   Alternative Hypothesis (H_A): $\mu \neq \mu$
   Blscore Glscore
3. Frequency Distribution: Normal
4. Type of Paradigm: Pre-Experimental
5. Confidence Interval:95%
   Population: 100 and Level of Significance: $\alpha=0.05$
6. Sample Size: 25
7. Categories: A, B, C and D
8. Treatment: Four Group Design with Simple Treatment.

9. Test: t – Test (Four test)
10. No. of Tails: Two – tailed
    If H=0, Accept H_0 Else H_A

Paradigm –II

1. Claim The New Orientation Programmes Imporve the Employee Productivity.]
2. Null Hypothesis:
   $H_0: \mu_1 = \mu_2$
   Alternative Hypothesis:
   H_A: The pre-test and post-test score differ $\mu_1 < \mu_2$
3. Frequency Distribution: Normal
4. Type of Paradigm: Using
   Internal Evidence
5. Confidence Interval:95%
   Significance:0.05
6. Population:100
   Sample Size: 25
   Research Design:Before-and –After
   Without Control Design
7. Catogeries: Only Category –A
   Emloyees
8. Treatment: New Orientation
   Programme
9. Tests: t- Test
10. Number of Tails: Paired two tailed Test

Paradigm III

1. Claim: Ten –Criteria OP does not influence the Productivity.
2. Null Hypothesis: $\mu C1 = \mu C2 = \mu C3 = \mu C4 = \mu C5 = \mu C6 = \mu C7 = \mu C8 = \mu C9 = \mu 10$
   Aletrnative Hypothesis: $\mu C1 \neq \mu C2 \neq \mu C3 \neq \mu C4 \neq \mu C5 \neq \mu C6 \neq \mu C7 \neq \mu C8 \neq \mu C9 \neq \mu C10$

3. Frequency Distribution: Normal
4. Type of Paradigm: True Experimental Design with External Evidence
5. Confidence Interanl:95%
   Significance:0.05
6. Population:100
   Sample Size: 50 (25X2)
   Simple Factorial Research Design
7. Categories: Category A & Category B
8. Treament: Ten –Point Criteria Training Programme.
9. Test: 2-Way ANOVA
10. Number of Tails: Two-tailed.

Paradigm-IV

1. Claim: Two – Models are compared to test their yield
2. Null Hypothesis $\mu M1 = \mu M2$
   Alternative Hypothesis: $\mu M1 \neq \mu M2$
3. Frequency Distribution: Normal
4. Type of Paradigm: True Experimental Design to Compare Algorithms (Cluster Procedures)
5. Confidence Internal: 95%
   Significance: 0.05
6. Population: 100
   Sample Size:(25X4)
   Research Design: Simple Matrix
7. Categories: A, B, C and D.
8. Treatment: Cluster Procedures 1)Single 2) Complete 3) Average 4) Centroid
9. Test: t-Test
10. Number of Tails: Two- tailed.
    h=t-test 2(X, Y, 0.05, 'both')

Natural Behavior Computing is used to find Hierarchical Clusters based on Human Nature. Human Nature is assessed using Ten Attributes(Criteria required for Behaviour Computing).

This problem is solved using graph-representation method which is having Adjacency matrix.

The vertices of the graph represent the ten-point criteria.
The first criteria Morality is not represented in the graph.
Breadth-first search is used in the graph.
Morality is the input(if Morality Code ==1) follow evaluating sequence->

1. Truth	2. Wisdom	3. Effort
4. Generosity	5. Determination	6. Patience
7. Loving-kindness	8. Renunciation	9. Equanimity

By informal interview method and observation all the employees were found to have missing score of Attribute Code 8 and 9.(Therefore only first SEVEN Criteria are considered,)

IDEAL CONDITIONS FOR UNIVERSITY ERP-HR HUMAN NATURE COMPUTING MODULE THE FOLLOWING TEN CRITERIA ARE EXPECTED FOR IMPROVED PRODUCTIVITY BASED ON AFFECTIVE DOMAIN:

1. Morality
2. Truth
3. Wisdom
4. Effort
5. Generesity
6. Detetrmination
7. Patience
8. Loving Kindness
9. Renunciation ----- Not Observed in individual behaviour
10. Equanimity ----- Not Observed in individual behaviour

	Generosity	Patience	Determination	wisdom	Loving Kindness	Effort	Truth
Generosity	0	1	1	1	0	0	0
Patience	1	0	1	0	0	0	0
Determination	1	1	0	0	1	1	0
wisdom	1	0	0	0	0	1	0
Loving Kindness	0	0	1	0	0	0	0
Effort	0	0	1	1	0	0	1
Truth	0	0	0	0	0	1	0

Breadth -First Search

Breadth -First Search is used to initialize the Adjacency Matrix in the code to connect two points of the graph together.

First, each entry represents the presence or absence of an edge between the two vertices of the graph.

Secondly, adjacency matrices are sparse and there is a wastage of storage space because this is a sparse matrix there are more zeros than ones.

Since breadth-first search specifies the least recently visited vertices as the vertex from which we visit all the unvisited adjacent vertices.

Two Questionnaires are used as Research Instrument for Data Collection

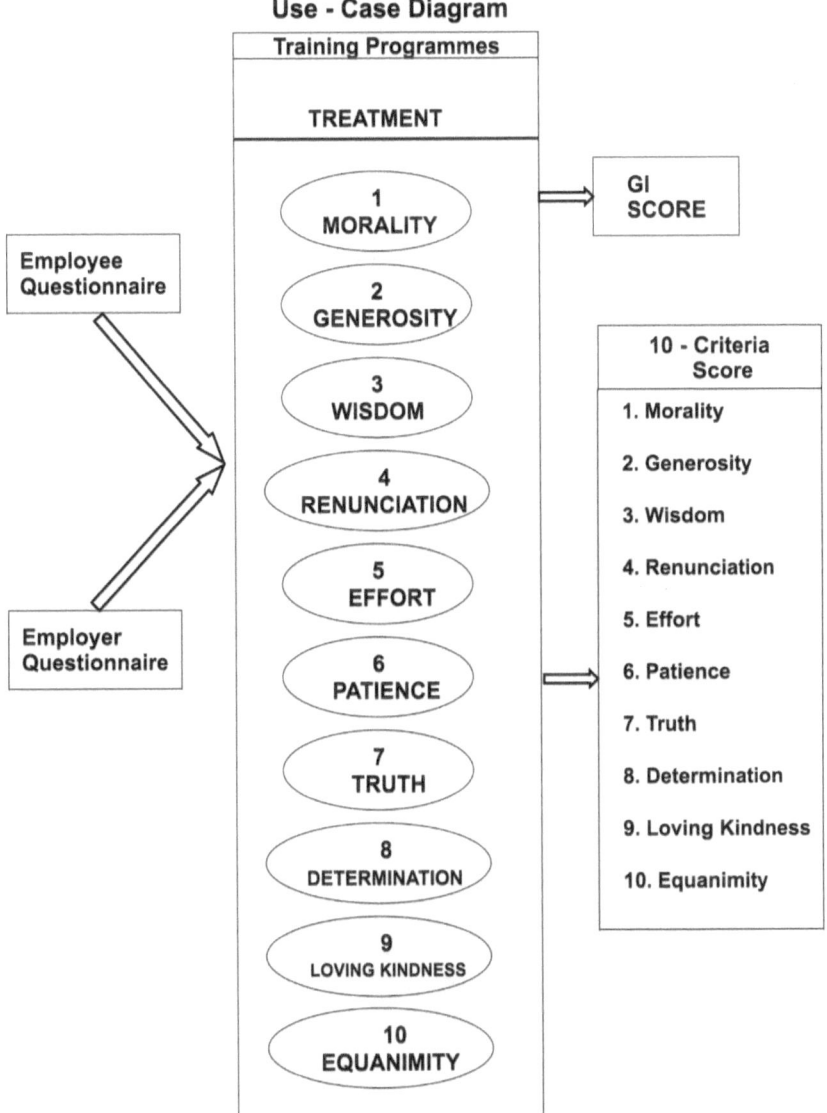

Fig. 2 : Use – Case Diagram for Behavior Computing Function

Final BI Score is Computed by adding the Ten Criteria Scores.

Query Operator Graph

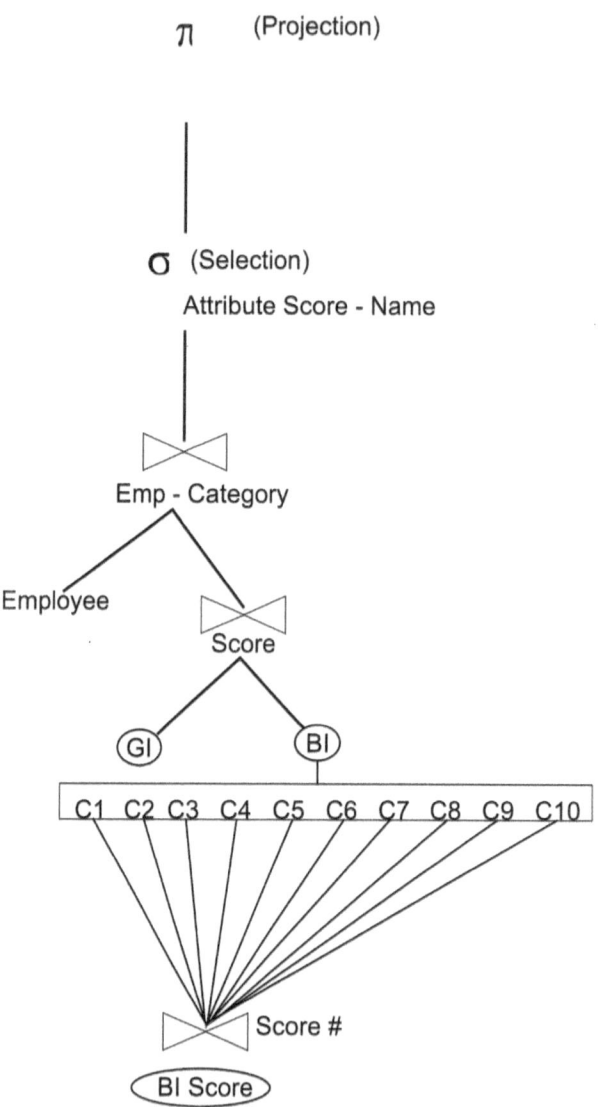

Fig. 3 : Query Operator Graph

Breadth-First Search Algorithm is used to find individual scores of Employees

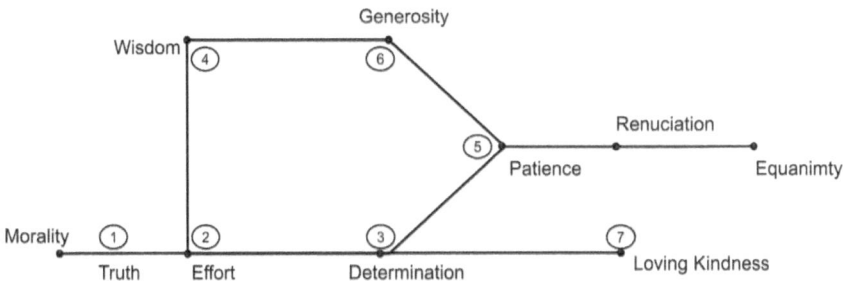

Fig. 4 : Breadth-First Search used in the graph

Traversal pattern of graph which is the indicator of an individual's Linearly connected Attribute Scores

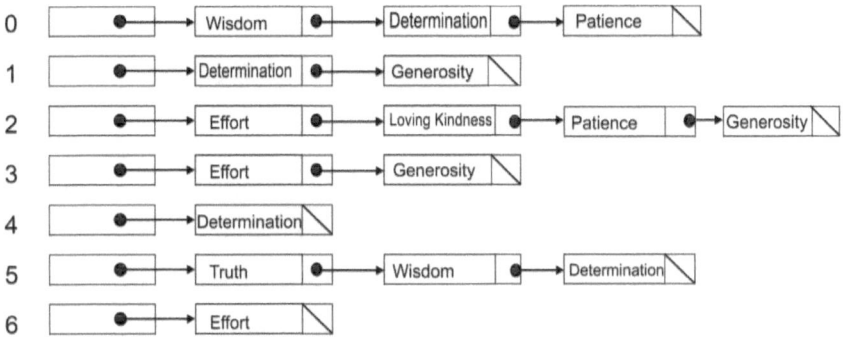

Fig. 5 : Graph representing Adjacency lists

The HR-model created is essentially useful for measuring employee productivity.

But besides measuring employee productivity this computational component would be extremely useful for:

(1) Providing preferred staffing arrangements for achieving high employee productivity.
(2) Useful as a manpower planning system in reducing costs.
(3) Finding and locating staff expertise or for work-capacity evaluation.
(4) It would be useful for assigning a standby duty.
(5) Restricting business workflow by restricting organizational structure.
(6) Providing a better Job design.
(7) Management of Time-Series data of Employees s
(8) For providing quality work.

1.14 Cluster Analysis:

Cluster Analysis is used as the Research Methodology.
Data used:

Data of 100 employees is collected from the University Organization.

DATA COLLECTION AND SAMPLING:

Data is collected using the score of BI and GI variables based on the precept score. Stratified Population of 100 Employees is choosen for the study. Stratified Random Sampling is used in the study with a sample size of 25 Employees.

DATA OF CATEGORY- A EMPLOYEES

X = [4 4;1 2;4 4;4 4; 4 4;4 3;5 5;3 3;4 4;3 3;4 4;3 2;
2 2;2 2;5 5;2 3;4 4;3 2;5 5;3 3;2 2;5 5;4 4;4 4;
3 3]

DATA OF CATEGORY- B EMPLOYEES

X = [3 3;4 4;3 2;2 3;5 5;3 3;2 2;4 3;4 4;2 2;5 5;3 3;
4 4;4 4;3 3;2 2;3 2;2 3;1 2;2 2;4 3;3 4;4 4;3 4;
3 4]

DATA OF CATEGORY- C EMPLOYEES

X = [1 1;1 1;5 5;3 3;1 1;1 1; 1 1;4 4;5 5;3 3;1 1;1 1;
2 2;2 2; 2 2;1 2;2 1;2 2;3 3;4 4;2 2;1 2;5 5;3 3; 4 4]

DATA OF CATEGORY- D EMPLOYEES

X = [1 1;1 1;2 1; 2 1;1 2;4 4;2 1;1 2;1 1;2 3;2 3;1 1;
3 3;2 2;2 2;1 1;2 2;4 4;1 1;1 1;2 2;2 2; 2 2;1 1;
2 2]

3.3. TABLES USED IN THE STUDY:

The following Rule-Base is used to evaluate the GI measurement.

Table 1: Rule – Base for BI

S.No.	Precept	Absence – 0 Presence – 1
1	P1: Abstinence from Killing	0/1
2	P2: Abstinence from taking what is not given	0/1
3	P3: Abstinence from Sexual Misconduct	0/1
4	P4: Abstinence from false speech	0/1
5	P5: Abstinence from intoxicating drinks and drugs	0/1

By using the precept measurement a Behavioral Integrity Score Matrix is generated.

Table 2: BI Score Matrix (Samples)

Emp.	P1	P2	P3	P4	P5	Total
Emp1-A	1	1	1	1	1	5
Emp2-B	1	1	0	1	0	3
Emp3-C	1	1	0	0	0	2
Emp4-D	1	1	0	0	0	2

A - Category 'A' Employee
B - Category 'B' Employee
C - Category 'C' Employee
D - Category 'D' Employee

Table 3: Likert Scale

S.No.	GI Score	Grade	Numeric Value
1	> = 85 (Outstanding)	A	5
2	84 = 70 (Very Good)	B	4
3	69-61 (Good)	C	3
4	60-40 (Average)	D	2
5	< 40 (Below Average	E	1

1.15 Computational Processing Steps:

Matrix Processing Software is used to define the two dimensional matrix. The computational processing is performed using the following steps:

Step 1: A matrix called X is generated with 10 – objects treated as 10 – employees. The values of BI and GI are inputted in the 10-objects. An example matrix is defined as follows:
X = [5 5; 4 4; 2 3; 1 1; 5 5; 3 2; 2 2; 1 2; 1 1; 3 2]

Step 2: The pair-wise distance is computed for individual employee.
Y = pdist(X)

Step 3: The squareform is generated by using the function:
squareform(Y)

Step 4: The linkage between the clusters is computed.
Z = linkage (Y)

Step 5: We then find the cophenetic correlation coefficient which is used to verify the dissimilarity amongst the two variables Z and Y using the function cophenet.
c= cophene (Z, Y). We obtain the value of c = 0.9024

Step 6: Cophenetic correlation is Computed as follows:

1) Pairwise distance between the object based on the 'cityblock' metric and
2) Create agglomerative hierarchical cluster tree by using un-weighted average distance (UPGMA) – by using 'average' method of cluster computation.
   Y = pdist (X, ' cityblock');
   Z = linkage (Y, 'average');
   c= cophenet (Z, Y)
   We obtain c = 0.9131 as the result.

Step 7: Verification of consistency co-efficient is done.
We compute the in-consistency co-efficient.
I = inconsistent (Z)

Table 5: Values of inconsistency co-efficient

Mean	Standard Deviation	No. Of Links	Inconsistency Co-efficient
0	0	1	0
0	0	1	0
0	0	1	0
0.5000	0.7071	2	0.7071
0.5000	0.7071	2	0.7071
0.5000	0.7071	2	0.7071
1.3333	0.4714	2	0.7071
1.6944	0.7087	3	1.0190
3.1230	2.5506	3	1.1093

Step 8: - To find the Natural Divisions in Data.
If we lower the inconsistency co-efficient threshold to 0.8 and we use the function cluster which is used to find the natural divisions in data
T= cluster (Z, 'cutoff', 0.8).

COMPARISON OF TWO EMPLOYEE CATEGORIES ON THE BASIS OF TEN-FACTOR-CRITERIA

ANOVA for Balanced Design

A two way ANOVA test is used to perform a balanced two-way ANOVA for comparing the means of ten columns and fifty rows of the obtained scores in the Matrix.

The data in different columns is column factor A which is used to represent the TEN-FACTOR-CRITERIA (Moralilty, Genrosity, Renunciation, Wisdom, Effort, Patience, Truthfulness, Determination, Loving Kindness, Equanimity) Score values pertaining to ten parameters obtained by the 50 Employees(25 Employees of Category-A and 25 Employees of Category-B) based on the Score obtained using Questionnaire I and II(Appendix).

The Management awards the Score using two Questionnaire outputs considered together. The maximum score is 10 marks.

Research Design – Simple Factorial 10x2 Research Design is used for the Experimental Study.

The data in different rows represent changes in row factor B(Category–A, Category-B) which has two levels for two employee categories. The first 25 rows represents data of Category-A Employees and the remaining rows represent data of Category-B Employees.

Main Hypothesis:

H_0: There is no variance in the Ten-Factor-Score obtained by two employee types.
H_A: There is variance in the Ten-Factor-Score obtained by two employee types.

Inference:

ANOVA Table is used to draw the following inference from the two way ANOVA test.

If any p value is near zero, this casts doubt on the associated null hypothesis. A sufficiently small p value for H_{0A} suggests that at least one column-sample mean is significantly different than the other column-sample means; i.e., there is a main effect due to factor A.

Statistical Significance:

A sufficiently small p value for H_{0B} suggests that at least one row-sample mean is significantly different than the other row-sample means; i.e., there is a main effect due to factor B.

Interaction between the two factors:

A sufficiently small p value for H_{0AB} suggests that there is an interaction between factors A and B. The choice of a limit for the p value to determine whether a result is "statistically significant" is left to the researcher. It is common to declare a result significant if the p value is less than 0.05 or 0.01.

Experiment –Two-way ANOVA Test

% Two-way ANOVA test
C = [7 8 6 6 7 7 8 8 8;
 7 7 6 6 5 4 6 7 5 7;
 8 5 5 4 5 6 5 5 5 5;
 7 8 7 8 6 5 8 8 6 7;
 7 7 7 8 8 6 6 7 5 6;
 8 7 7 7 8 7 6 8 8 8;
 5 6 5 6 5 6 5 8 5 6;
 6 5 5 5 5 6 5 4 5 6;
 8 7 6 7 6 7 7 8 8 7;
 7 7 7 6 6 5 5 6 7 7;
 6 6 5 5 4 5 5 5 6 5;
 5 1 4 3 4 4 5 4 2 2;
 4 3 5 4 3 3 2 3 2 2;
 3 3 3 4 3 4 2 2 2 1;
 2 1 1 2 3 3 2 2 2 1;
 8 7 7 7 8 7 8 7 8 8;
 8 8 7 8 8 7 8 6 7 7;
 8 8 7 7 7 8 7 8 7 6;
 8 8 8 7 7 8 8 7 8 7;
 8 8 8 6 7 6 7 8 8 8;
 7 8 6 6 7 7 6 8 8 8;
 8 7 6 8 7 7 7 8 7 8;
 7 7 6 6 5 6 7 7 7 8;
 8 8 6 7 6 5 6 8 8 7;
 7 7 6 7 6 6 5 7 7 7;
 8 8 7 6 7 5 6 8 8 8;

```
6 6 5 4 4 5 4 6 5 6;
5 5 4 3 4 4 4 5 5 5;
4 4 3 3 2 1 3 4 3 2;
4 4 3 2 1 2 3 4 4 4;
4 5 2 1 2 1 2 4 5 4;
4 5 4 3 4 4 4 5 5 3;
4 2 3 4 4 3 4 3 5 5;
7 6 5 4 5 6 5 6 6 5;
7 7 4 3 7 5 6 7 6 7;
5 5 3 2 4 4 3 5 4 5;
4 4 3 2 3 4 4 4 4 3;
3 3 3 2 2 1 2 3 2 3;
7 7 6 6 6 6 7 7 7 6;
6 7 5 6 6 5 6 6 7 6;
6 6 6 5 6 5 5 6 6 6;
6 5 5 4 5 5 4 5 6 7;
5 5 4 3 5 3 4 5 4 6;
5 4 4 3 4 4 4 5 4 5;
4 4 3 4 3 3 2 4 3 2;
3 2 2 2 3 1 2 3 3 3;
2 3 2 2 1 2 2 2 3 2;
5 5 4 4 3 4 4 5 6 5;
6 6 5 6 5 5 6 6 6 7;
7 7 6 7 6 7 6 6 7 7];
```

E = 10;/*Number of Criteria*/
[p,tbl,stats] = anova2(C,E);

Data Processing of Category A Employees

CHAPTER - II

CHAPTER 2

DATA PROCESSING OF CATEGORY A EMPLOYEES

2.1 Method-1: 'euclidean' and 'average'

Step 1: Define the Matrix
X = [4 4;1 2;4 4;4 4;4 4;3;5 5;3 3;4 4;3 3;4 4;3 2;
    2;2 2;5 5;2 3;4 4;3 2;5 5;3 3;2 2;5 5;4 4;4 4;3 3]

Step 2: Find the Distance Information
Y = pdist (X)

Step 3: Generate the Squareform
squareform(Y)

Step 4: Find the Pairwise Distance
Y = pdist(X,'euclidean')

Step 5: Find the Cluster Linkage
Z = linkage(Y,'average')

Step 6: Determine cophenetic correlation coefficient
c = cophenet(Z,Y)

Step 7: Construct the Dendrogram
dendrogram(Z)

Output:
c = 0.7126

2.2 Method-2: 'euclidean' and 'centroid'

Step 1: Define the Matrix
X = [4 4;1 2;4 4;4 4;4 4;4 3;5 5;3 3;4 4;3 3;4 4;3 2;
   2 2;2 2;5 5;2 3;4 4;3 2;5 5;3 3;2 2;5 5;4 4;4 4;3 3]

Step 2: Find the Distance Information
Y = pdist(X)
Step 3: Generate the Squareform
squareform(Y)

Step 4: Find the Pairwise Distance
Y = pdist(X,'euclidean')

Step 5: Find the Cluster Linkage
Z = linkage(Y,'centroid')

Step 6: Determine cophenetic correlation coefficient
c = cophenet(Z,Y)

Step 7: Construct the Dendrogram
dendrogram(Z)

Output:
c = 0.7882

2.3 Method-3: 'euclidean' and 'complete'

Step 1: Define the Matrix
X = [4 4;1 2;4 4;4 4;4 4;4 3;5 5;3 3;4 4;3 3;4 4;3 2;
      2 2;2 2;5 5;2 3;4 4;3 2;5 5;3 3;2 2;5 5;4 4;4 4;3 3]

Step 2: Find the Distance Information
Y = pdist(X)

Step 3: Generate the Squareform
squareform(Y)

Step 4: Find the Pairwise Distance
Y = pdist(X,'euclidean')

Step 5: Find the Cluster Linkage
Z = linkage(Y,'complete')

Step 6: Determine cophenetic correlation coefficient
c = cophenet(Z,Y)

Step 7: Construct the Dendrogram
dendrogram(Z)

Output:
c = 0.7810

2.4 Method-4: 'euclidean' and 'median'

Step 1: Define the Matrix
X = [4 4;1 2;4 4;4 4;4 4;4 3;5 5;3 3;4 4;3 3;4 4;3 2;
 2 2;2 2;5 5;2 3;4 4;3 2;5 5;3 3;2 2;5 5;4 4;4 4;3 3]

Step 2: Find the Distance Information
Y = pdist(X)

Step 3: Generate the Squareform
squareform(Y)

Step 4: Find the Pairwise Distance
Y = pdist(X,'euclidean')

Step 5: Find the Cluster Linkage
Z = linkage(Y,'median')

Step 6: Determine cophenetic correlation coefficient
c = cophenet(Z,Y)

Step 7: Construct the Dendrogram
dendrogram(Z)

Output:
c = 0.7432

2.5 Method-5: Euclidean and Single

Step 1: Define the Matrix
X = [4 4;1 2;4 4;4 4;4 4;4 3;5 5;3 3;4 4;3 3;4 4;3 2;
2 2;2 2;5 5;2 3;4 4;3 2;5 5;3 3;2 2;5 5;4 4;4 4;3 3]

Step 2: Find the Distance Information
Y = pdist(X)

Step 3: Generate the Squareform
squareform(Y)

Step 4: Find the Pairwise Distance
Y = pdist(X,'euclidean')

Step 5: Find the Cluster Linkage
Z = linkage(Y,'single')

Step 6: Determine cophenetic correlation coefficient
c = cophenet(Z,Y)

Step 7: Construct the Dendrogram
dendrogram(Z)

Output:
c = 0.7126

2.6 Method-6: Euclidean and Ward

Step 1: Define the Matrix
X = [4 4;1 2;4 4;4 4;4 4;4 3;5 5;3 3;4 4;3 3;4 4;3 2;
    2 2;2 2;5 5;2 3;4 4;3 2;5 5;3 3;2 2;5 5;4 4;4 4;3 3]

Step 2: Find the Distance Information
Y = pdist(X)

Step 3: Generate the Squareform
squareform(Y)

Step 4: Find the Pairwise Distance
Y = pdist(X,'euclidean')

Step 5: Find the Cluster Linkage
Z = linkage(Y,'ward')

Step 6: Determine cophenetic correlation coefficient
c = cophenet(Z,Y)

Step 7: Construct the Dendrogram
dendrogram(Z)

Output:
c = 0.7676

2.7 Method-7: Euclidean and weighted

Step 1: Define the Matrix
X = [4 4;1 2;4 4;4 4;4 4;4 3;5 5;3 3;4 4;3 3;4 4;3 2;
    2 2;2 2;5 5;2 3;4 4;3 2;5 5;3 3;2 2;5 5;4 4;4 4;3 3]

Step 2: Find the Distance Information
Y = pdist(X)

Step 3: Generate the Squareform
squareform(Y)

Step 4: Find the Pairwise Distance
Y = pdist(X,'euclidean')

Step 5: Find the Cluster Linkage
Z = linkage(Y,'weighted')

Step 6: Determine cophenetic correlation coefficient
c = cophenet(Z,Y)

Step 7: Construct the Dendrogram
dendrogram(Z)

Output:
c = 0.7969

2.8 Method-8: Chebychev and average

Step 1: Define the Matrix
X = [4 4;1 2;4 4;4 4;4 4;4 3;5 5;3 3;4 4;3 3;4 4;3 2;
    2 2;2 2;5 5;2 3;4 4;3 2;5 5;3 3;2 2;5 5;4 4;4 4;3 3]

Step 2: Find the Distance Information
Y = pdist(X)

Step 3: Generate the Squareform
squareform(Y)

Step 4: Find the Pairwise Distance
Y = pdist(X,'chebychev')

Step 5: Find the Cluster Linkage
Z = linkage(Y,'average')

Step 6: Determine cophenetic correlation coefficient
c = cophenet(Z,Y)

Step 7: Construct the Dendrogram
dendrogram(Z)

Output:
c = 0.8178

2.9 Method-9: Mahalanobis and average

Step 1: Define the Matrix
X = [4 4;1 2;4 4;4 4;4 4;4 3;5 5;3 3;4 4;3 3;4 4;3 2;
    2 2;2 2;5 5;2 3;4 4;3 2;5 5;3 3;2 2;5 5;4 4;4 4;3 3]

Step 2: Find the Distance Information
Y = pdist(X)

Step 3: Generate the Squareform
squareform(Y)

Step 4: Find the Pairwise Distance
Y = pdist(X,'mahalanobis')

Step 5: Find the Cluster Linkage
Z = linkage(Y,'average')

Step 6: Determine cophenetic correlation coefficient
c = cophenet(Z,Y)

Step 7: Construct the Dendrogram
dendrogram(Z)

Output:
c = 0.9080

2.10 Method-10: Cosine and average

Step 1: Define the Matrix
X = [4 4;1 2;4 4;4 4;4 4;4 3;5 5;3 3;4 4;3 3;4 4;3 2;
 2 2;2 2;5 5;2 3;4 4;3 2;5 5;3 3;2 2;5 5;4 4;4 4;3 3]

Step 2: Find the Distance Information
Y = pdist(X)

Step 3: Generate the Squareform
squareform(Y)

Step 4: Find the Pairwise Distance
Y = pdist(X,'cosine')

Step 5: Find the Cluster Linkage
Z = linkage(Y,'average')

Step 6: Determine cophenetic correlation coefficient
c = cophenet(Z,Y)

Step 7: Construct the Dendrogram
dendrogram(Z)

Output:
c = 0.8187

2.11 Method-11: Cityblock and average

Step 1: Define the Matrix
X = [4 4;1 2;4 4;4 4;4 4;4 3;5 5;3 3;4 4;3 3;4 4;3 2;
 2 2;2 2;5 5;2 3;4 4;3 2;5 5;3 3;2 2;5 5;4 4;4 4;3 3]

Step 2: Find the Distance Information
Y = pdist(X)

Step 3: Generate the Squareform
squareform(Y)

Step 4: Find the Pairwise Distance
Y = pdist(X,'cityblock')

Step 5: Find the Cluster Linkage
Z = linkage(Y,'average')

Step 6: Determine cophenetic correlation coefficient
c = cophenet(Z,Y)

Step 7: Construct the Dendrogram
dendrogram(Z)

Output:
c = 0.7803

2.12 Method-12: Seuclidean and single

Step 1: Define the Matrix
X = [4 4;1 2;4 4;4 4;4 4;4 3;5 5;3 3;4 4;3 3;4 4;3 2;
2 2;2 2;5 5;2 3;4 4;3 2;5 5;3 3;2 2;5 5;4 4;4 4;3 3]

Step 2: Find the Distance Information
Y = pdist(X)

Step 3: Generate the Squareform
squareform(Y)

Step 4: Find the Pairwise Distance
Y = pdist(X,'seuclidean')

Step 5: Find the Cluster Linkage
Z = linkage(Y,'single')

Step 6: Determine cophenetic correlation coefficient
c = cophenet(Z,Y)

Step 7: Construct the Dendrogram
dendrogram(Z)

Output:
c = 0.7170

2.13 Method-13: cityblock and single

Step 1: Define the Matrix
X = [4 4;1 2;4 4;4 4;4 4;4 3;5 5;3 3;4 4;3 3;4 4;3 2;
2 2;2 2;5 5;2 3;4 4;3 2;5 5;3 3;2 2;5 5;4 4;4 4;3 3]

Step 2: Find the Distance Information
Y = pdist(X)

Step 3: Generate the Squareform
squareform(Y)

Step 4: Find the Pairwise Distance
Y = pdist(X,'cityblock')

Step 5: Find the Cluster Linkage
Z = linkage(Y,'single')

Step 6: Determine cophenetic correlation coefficient
c = cophenet(Z,Y)

Step 7: Construct the Dendrogram
dendrogram(Z)

Output:
c = 0.6723

2.14 Method-14: Hamming and average

Step 1: Define the Matrix
X = [4 4;1 2;4 4;4 4;4 4;4 3;5 5;3 3;4 4;3 3;4 4;3 2;
　　2 2;2 2;5 5;2 3;4 4;3 2;5 5;3 3;2 2;5 5;4 4;4 4;3 3]

Step 2: Find the Distance Information
Y = pdist(X)

Step 3: Generate the Squareform
squareform(Y)

Step 4: Find the Pairwise Distance
Y = pdist(X,'hamming')

Step 5: Find the Cluster Linkage
Z = linkage(Y,'average')

Step 6: Determine cophenetic correlation coefficient
c = cophenet(Z,Y)

Step 7: Construct the Dendrogram
dendrogram(Z)

Output:
c = 0.9638

2.15 Method-15: Jaccard and average

Step 1: Define the Matrix
X = [4 4;1 2;4 4;4 4;4 4;4 3;5 5;3 3;4 4;3 3;4 4;3 2;
   2 2;2 2;5 5;2 3;4 4;3 2;5 5;3 3;2 2;5 5;4 4;4 4;3 3]

Step 2: Find the Distance Information
Y = pdist(X)

Step 3: Generate the Squareform
squareform(Y)

Step 4: Find the Pairwise Distance
Y = pdist(X,'jaccard')

Step 5: Find the Cluster Linkage
Z = linkage(Y,'average')

Step 6: Determine cophenetic correlation coefficient
c = cophenet(Z,Y)

Step 7: Construct the Dendrogram
dendrogram(Z)

Output:
c = 0.9638

2.16 Method-16: seuclidean and centroid

Step 1: Define the Matrix
X = [4 4;1 2;4 4;4 4;4 4;4 4;3;5 5;3 3;4 4;3 3;4 4;3 2;
    2 2;2 2;5 5;2 3;4 4;3 2;5 5;3 3;2 2;5 5;4 4;4 4;3 3]

Step 2: Find the Distance Information
Y = pdist(X)

Step 3: Generate the Squareform
squareform(Y)

Step 4: Find the Pairwise Distance
Y = pdist(X,'seuclidean')

Step 5: Find the Cluster Linkage
Z = linkage(Y,'centroid')

Step 6: Determine cophenetic correlation coefficient
c = cophenet(Z,Y)

Step 7: Construct the Dendrogram
dendrogram(Z)

Output:
c =0.7901

2.17 Method-17: cityblock and centroid

Step 1: Define the Matrix
X = [4 4;1 2;4 4;4 4;4 4;4 3;5 5;3 3;4 4;3 3;4 4;3 2;
2 2;2 2;5 5;2 3;4 4;3 2;5 5;3 3;2 2;5 5;4 4;4 4;3 3]

Step 2: Find the Distance Information
Y = pdist(X)

Step 3: Generate the Squareform
squareform(Y)

Step 4: Find the Pairwise Distance
Y = pdist(X,'cityblock')

Step 5: Find the Cluster Linkage
Z = linkage(Y,'centroid')

Step 6: Determine cophenetic correlation coefficient
c = cophenet(Z,Y)

Step 7: Construct the Dendrogram
dendrogram(Z)

Output:
c = 0.7802

2.18 Method-18: Minkowski and centroid

Step 1: Define the Matrix
X = [4 4;1 2;4 4;4 4;4 4;4 3;5 5;3 3;4 4;3 3;4 4;3 2;
 2 2;2 2;5 5;2 3;4 4;3 2;5 5;3 3;2 2;5 5;4 4;4 4;3 3]

Step 2: Find the Distance Information
Y = pdist(X)

Step 3: Generate the Squareform
squareform(Y)

Step 4: Find the Pairwise Distance
Y = pdist(X,'minkowski')

Step 5: Find the Cluster Linkage
Z = linkage(Y,'centroid')

Step 6: Determine cophenetic correlation coefficient
c = cophenet(Z,Y)

Step 7: Construct the Dendrogram
dendrogram(Z)

Output:
c = 0.7882

2.19 Method-19: chebychev and centroid

Step 1: Define the Matrix
X = [4 4;1 2;4 4;4 4;4 4;4 3;5 5;3 3;4 4;3 3;4 4;3 2;
     2 2;2 2;5 5;2 3;4 4;3 2;5 5;3 3;2 2;5 5;4 4;4 4;3 3]

Step 2: Find the Distance Information
Y = pdist(X)

Step 3: Generate the Squareform
squareform(Y)

Step 4: Find the Pairwise Distance
Y = pdist(X,'chebychev')

Step 5: Find the Cluster Linkage
Z = linkage(Y,'centroid')

Step 6: Determine cophenetic correlation coefficient
c = cophenet(Z,Y)

Step 7: Construct the Dendrogram
dendrogram(Z)

Output:
c = 0.8171

2.20 Method-20: Mahalanobis and centroid

Step 1: Define the Matrix
X = [4 4;1 2;4 4;4 4;4 4;4 3;5 5;3 3;4 4;3 3;4 4;3 2;
    2 2;2 2;5 5;2 3;4 4;3 2;5 5;3 3;2 2;5 5;4 4;4 4;3 3]

Step 2: Find the Distance Information
Y = pdist(X)

Step 3: Generate the Squareform
squareform(Y)

Step 4: Find the Pairwise Distance
Y = pdist(X,'mahalanobis')

Step 5: Find the Cluster Linkage
Z = linkage(Y,'centroid')

Step 6: Determine cophenetic correlation coefficient
c = cophenet(Z,Y)

Step 7: Construct the Dendrogram
dendrogram(Z)

Output:
c =0.9067

2.21 Method-21: Cosine and centroid

Step 1: Define the Matrix
X = [4 4;1 2;4 4;4 4;4 4;4 3;5 5;3 3;4 4;3 3;4 4;3 2;
2 2;2 2;5 5;2 3;4 4;3 2;5 5;3 3;2 2;5 5;4 4;4 4;3 3]

Step 2: Find the Distance Information
Y = pdist(X)

Step 3: Generate the Squareform
squareform(Y)

Step 4: Find the Pairwise Distance
Y = pdist(X,'cosine')

Step 5: Find the Cluster Linkage
Z = linkage(Y,'centroid')

Step 6: Determine cophenetic correlation coefficient
c = cophenet(Z,Y)

Step 7: Construct the Dendrogram
dendrogram(Z)

Output:
c = 0.8177

2.22 Method-22: Minkowski and single

Step 1: Define the Matrix
X = [4 4;1 2;4 4;4 4;4 4;4 3;5 5;3 3;4 4;3 3;4 4;3 2;
    2 2;2 2;5 5;2 3;4 4;3 2;5 5;3 3;2 2;5 5;4 4;4 4;3 3]

Step 2: Find the Distance Information
Y = pdist(X)

Step 3: Generate the Squareform
squareform(Y)

Step 4: Find the Pairwise Distance
Y = pdist(X,'minkowski')

Step 5: Find the Cluster Linkage
Z = linkage(Y,'single')

Step 6: Determine cophenetic correlation coefficient
c = cophenet(Z,Y)

Step 7: Construct the Dendrogram
dendrogram(Z)

Output:
c = 0.7126

2.23 Method-23: Mahalanobis and single

Step 1: Define the Matrix
X = [4 4;1 2;4 4;4 4;4 4;4 3;5 5;3 3;4 4;3 3;4 4;3 2;
    2 2;2 2;5 5;2 3;4 4;3 2;5 5;3 3;2 2;5 5;4 4;4 4;3 3]

Step 2: Find the Distance Information
Y = pdist(X)

Step 3: Generate the Squareform
squareform(Y)

Step 4: Find the Pairwise Distance
Y = pdist(X,'mahalanobis')

Step 5: Find the Cluster Linkage
Z = linkage(Y,'single')

Step 6: Determine cophenetic correlation coefficient
c = cophenet(Z,Y)

Step 7: Construct the Dendrogram
dendrogram(Z)

Output:
c = 0.8639

2.24 Method-24: Hamming and Centroid

Step 1: Define the Matrix
X = [4 4;1 2;4 4;4 4;4 4;4 3;5 5;3 3;4 4;3 3;4 4;3 2;
   2 2;2 2;5 5;2 3;4 4;3 2;5 5;3 3;2 2;5 5;4 4;4 4;3 3]

Step 2: Find the Distance Information
Y = pdist(X)

Step 3: Generate the Squareform
squareform(Y)

Step 4: Find the Pairwise Distance
Y = pdist(X,'hamming')

Step 5: Find the Cluster Linkage
Z = linkage(Y,'centroid')

Step 6: Determine cophenetic correlation coefficient
c = cophenet(Z,Y)

Step 7: Construct the Dendrogram
dendrogram(Z)

Output:
c =0.9504

2.25 Method-25: Jaccard and centroid

Step 1: Define the Matrix
X = [4 4;1 2;4 4;4 4;4 4;4 3;5 5;3 3;4 4;3 3;4 4;3 2;
    2 2;2 2;5 5;2 3;4 4;3 2;5 5;3 3;2 2;5 5;4 4;4 4;3 3]

Step 2: Find the Distance Information
Y = pdist(X)

Step 3: Generate the Squareform
squareform(Y)

Step 4: Find the Pairwise Distance
Y = pdist(X,'jaccard')

Step 5: Find the Cluster Linkage
Z = linkage(Y,'centroid')

Step 6: Determine cophenetic correlation coefficient
c = cophenet(Z,Y)

Step 7: Construct the Dendrogram
dendrogram(Z)

Output:
c = 0.9504

2.26 Method-26: Seuclidean and complete

Step 1: Define the Matrix
X = [4 4;1 2;4 4;4 4;4 4;4 3;5 5;3 3;4 4;3 3;4 4;3 2;
    2 2;2 2;5 5;2 3;4 4;3 2;5 5;3 3;2 2;5 5;4 4;4 4;3 3]

Step 2: Find the Distance Information
Y = pdist(X)

Step 3: Generate the Squareform
squareform(Y)

Step 4: Find the Pairwise Distance
Y = pdist(X,'seuclidean')

Step 5: Find the Cluster Linkage
Z = linkage(Y,'complete')

Step 6: Determine cophenetic correlation coefficient
c = cophenet(Z,Y)

Step 7: Construct the Dendrogram
dendrogram(Z)

Output:
c = 0.7820

2.27 Method-27: cityblock and complete

Step 1: Define the Matrix
X = [4 4;1 2;4 4;4 4;4 4;4 3;5 5;3 3;4 4;3 3;4 4;3 2;
2 2;2 2;5 5;2 3;4 4;3 2;5 5;3 3;2 2;5 5;4 4;4 4;3 3]

Step 2: Find the Distance Information
Y = pdist(X)

Step 3: Generate the Squareform
squareform(Y)

Step 4: Find the Pairwise Distance
Y = pdist(X,'cityblock')

Step 5: Find the Cluster Linkage
Z = linkage(Y,'complete')

Step 6: Determine cophenetic correlation coefficient
c = cophenet(Z,Y)

Step 7: Construct the Dendrogram
dendrogram(Z)

Output:
c = 0.7646

2.28 Method-28: Minkowski and complete

Step 1: Define the Matrix
X = [4 4;1 2;4 4;4 4;4 4;4 3;5 5;3 3;4 4;3 3;4 4;3 2;
　　2 2;2 2;5 5;2 3;4 4;3 2;5 5;3 3;2 2;5 5;4 4;4 4;3 3]

Step 2: Find the Distance Information
Y = pdist(X)

Step 3: Generate the Squareform
squareform(Y)

Step 4: Find the Pairwise Distance
Y = pdist(X,'minkowski')

Step 5: Find the Cluster Linkage
Z = linkage(Y,'complete')

Step 6: Determine cophenetic correlation coefficient
c = cophenet(Z,Y)

Step 7: Construct the Dendrogram
dendrogram(Z)

Output:
c = 0.7810

2.29 Method-29: chebychev and complete

Step 1: Define the Matrix
X = [4 4;1 2;4 4;4 4;4 4;4 3;5 5;3 3;4 4;3 3;4 4;3 2;
    2 2;2 2;5 5;2 3;4 4;3 2;5 5;3 3;2 2;5 5;4 4;4 4;3 3]

Step 2: Find the Distance Information
Y = pdist(X)

Step 3: Generate the Squareform
squareform(Y)

Step 4: Find the Pairwise Distance
Y = pdist(X,'chebychev')

Step 5: Find the Cluster Linkage
Z = linkage(Y,'complete')

Step 6: Determine cophenetic correlation coefficient
c = cophenet(Z,Y)

Step 7: Construct the Dendrogram
dendrogram(Z)

Output:
c =0.7642

2.30 Method-30: Mahalanobis and Complete

Step 1: Define the Matrix
X = [4 4;1 2;4 4;4 4;4 4;4 3;5 5;3 3;4 4;3 3;4 4;3 2;
 2 2;2 2;5 5;2 3;4 4;3 2;5 5;3 3;2 2;5 5;4 4;4 4;3 3]

Step 2: Find the Distance Information
Y = pdist(X)

Step 3: Generate the Squareform
squareform(Y)

Step 4: Find the Pairwise Distance
Y = pdist(X,'mahalanobis')

Step 5: Find the Cluster Linkage
Z = linkage(Y,'complete')

Step 6: Determine cophenetic correlation coefficient
c = cophenet(Z,Y)

Step 7: Construct the Dendrogram
dendrogram(Z)

Output:
c = 0.8134

Data Processing of Category B Employees

CHAPTER - III

CHAPTER 3

DATA PROCESSING OF CATEGORY B EMPLOYEES

3.1 Method-1: 'euclidean' and 'average'

Step 1: Define the Matrix
X = [4 4;1 2;4 4;4 4;4 4;3 5 5;3 3;4 4;3 3;4 4;3 2;
2 2;2 2;5 5;2 3;4 4;3 2;5 5;3 3;2 2;5 5;4 4;4 4;3 3]

Step 2: Find the Distance Information
Y = pdist(X)

Step 3: Generate the Squareform
squareform(Y)

Step 4: Find the Pairwise Distance
Y = pdist(X,'euclidean')

Step 5: Find the Cluster Linkage
Z = linkage(Y,'average')

Step 6: Determine cophenetic correlation coefficient
c = cophenet(Z,Y)

Step 7: Construct the Dendrogram
dendrogram(Z)

Output:
c = 0.7916

3.2 Method-2: 'euclidean' and 'centroid'

Step 1: Define the Matrix
X = [4 4;1 2;4 4;4 4;4 4;4 3;5 5;3 3;4 4;3 3;4 4;3 2;
 2 2;2 2;5 5;2 3;4 4;3 2;5 5;3 3;2 2;5 5;4 4;4 4;3 3]

Step 2: Find the Distance Information
Y = pdist(X)

Step 3: Generate the Squareform
squareform(Y)

Step 4: Find the Pairwise Distance
Y = pdist(X,'euclidean')

Step 5: Find the Cluster Linkage
Z = linkage(Y,'centroid')

Step 6: Determine cophenetic correlation coefficient
c = cophenet(Z,Y)

Step 7: Construct the Dendrogram
dendrogram(Z)

Output:
c = 0.7892

3.3 Method-3: 'euclidean' and 'median'

Step 1: Define the Matrix
X = [4 4;1 2;4 4;4 4;4 4;3 5 5;3 3;4 4;3 3;4 4;3 2;
    2 2;2 2;5 5;2 3;4 4;3 2;5 5;3 3;2 2;5 5;4 4;4 4;3 3]

Step 2: Find the Distance Information
Y = pdist(X)

Step 3: Generate the Squareform
squareform(Y)

Step 4: Find the Pairwise Distance
Y = pdist(X,'euclidean')

Step 5: Find the Cluster Linkage
Z = linkage(Y,'median')

Step 6: Determine cophenetic correlation coefficient
c = cophenet(Z,Y)

Step 7: Construct the Dendrogram
dendrogram(Z)

Output:
c = 0.7916

3.4 Method-4: 'euclidean' and 'ward'

Step 1: Define the Matrix
X = [4 4;1 2;4 4;4 4;4 4;4 3;5 5;3 3;4 4;3 3;4 4;3 2;
    2 2;2 2;5 5;2 3;4 4;3 2;5 5;3 3;2 2;5 5;4 4;4 4;3 3]

Step 2: Find the Distance Information
Y = pdist(X)

Step 3: Generate the Squareform
squareform(Y)

Step 4: Find the Pairwise Distance
Y = pdist(X,'euclidean')

Step 5: Find the Cluster Linkage
Z = linkage(Y,'ward')

Step 6: Determine cophenetic correlation coefficient
c = cophenet(Z,Y)

Step 7: Construct the Dendrogram
dendrogram(Z)

Output:
c = 0.6824

3.5 Method-5: 'seuclidean' and 'average'

Step 1: Define the Matrix
X = [4 4;1 2;4 4;4 4;4 4;4 3;5 5;3 3;4 4;3 3;4 4;3 2;
    2 2;2 2;5 5;2 3;4 4;3 2;5 5;3 3;2 2;5 5;4 4;4 4;3 3]

Step 2: Find the Distance Information
Y = pdist(X)

Step 3: Generate the Squareform
squareform(Y)

Step 4: Find the Pairwise Distance
Y = pdist(X,'seuclidean')

Step 5: Find the Cluster Linkage
Z = linkage(Y,'average')

Step 6: Determine cophenetic correlation coefficient
c = cophenet(Z,Y)

Step 7: Construct the Dendrogram
dendrogram(Z)

Output:
c = 0.7306

3.6 Method-6: 'cityblock' and 'average'

Step 1: Define the Matrix
X = [4 4;1 2;4 4;4 4;4 4;4 3;5 5;3 3;4 4;3 3;4 4;3 2;
    2 2;2 2;5 5;2 3;4 4;3 2;5 5;3 3;2 2;5 5;4 4;4 4;3 3]

Step 2: Find the Distance Information
Y = pdist(X)

Step 3: Generate the Squareform
squareform(Y)

Step 4: Find the Pairwise Distance
Y = pdist(X,'cityblock')

Step 5: Find the Cluster Linkage
Z = linkage(Y,'average')

Step 6: Determine cophenetic correlation coefficient
c = cophenet(Z,Y)

Step 7: Construct the Dendrogram
dendrogram(Z)

Output:
c = 0.7793

3.7 Method-7: 'minkowski' and 'average'

Step 1: Define the Matrix
X = [4 4;1 2;4 4;4 4;4 4;4 3;5 5;3 3;4 4;3 3;4 4;3 2;
     2 2;2 2;5 5;2 3;4 4;3 2;5 5;3 3;2 2;5 5;4 4;4 4;3 3]

Step 2: Find the Distance Information
Y = pdist(X)

Step 3: Generate the Squareform
squareform(Y)

Step 4: Find the Pairwise Distance
Y = pdist(X,'minkowski')

Step 5: Find the Cluster Linkage
Z = linkage(Y,'average')

Step 6: Determine cophenetic correlation coefficient
c = cophenet(Z,Y)

Step 7: Construct the Dendrogram
dendrogram(Z)

Output:
c = 0.7916

3.8 Method-8: chebychev and average

Step 1: Define the Matrix
X = [4 4;1 2;4 4;4 4;4 4;4 3;5 5;3 3;4 4;3 3;4 4;3 2;
 2 2;2 2;5 5;2 3;4 4;3 2;5 5;3 3;2 2;5 5;4 4;4 4;3 3]

Step 2: Find the Distance Information
Y = pdist(X)

Step 3: Generate the Squareform
squareform(Y)

Step 4: Find the Pairwise Distance
Y = pdist(X,'chebychev')

Step 5: Find the Cluster Linkage
Z = linkage(Y,'average')

Step 6: Determine cophenetic correlation coefficient
c = cophenet(Z,Y)

Step 7: Construct the Dendrogram
dendrogram(Z)

Output:
c = 0.7602

3.9 Method-9: Mahalanobis and average

Step 1: Define the Matrix
X = [4 4;1 2;4 4;4 4;4 4;4 3;5 5;3 3;4 4;3 3;4 4;3 2;
    2 2;2 2;5 5;2 3;4 4;3 2;5 5;3 3;2 2;5 5;4 4;4 4;3 3]

Step 2: Find the Distance Information
Y = pdist(X)

Step 3: Generate the Squareform
squareform(Y)

Step 4: Find the Pairwise Distance
Y = pdist(X,'mahalanobis')

Step 5: Find the Cluster Linkage
Z = linkage(Y,'average')

Step 6: Determine cophenetic correlation coefficient
c = cophenet(Z,Y)

Step 7: Construct the Dendrogram
dendrogram(Z)

Output:
c = 0.7756

3.10 Method-10: Cosine and average

Step 1: Define the Matrix
X = [4 4;1 2;4 4;4 4;4 4;4 3;5 5;3 3;4 4;3 3;4 4;3 2;
   2 2;2 2;5 5;2 3;4 4;3 2;5 5;3 3;2 2;5 5;4 4;4 4;3 3]

Step 2: Find the Distance Information
Y = pdist(X)

Step 3: Generate the Squareform
squareform(Y)

Step 4: Find the Pairwise Distance
Y = pdist(X,'cosine')

Step 5: Find the Cluster Linkage
Z = linkage(Y,'average')

Step 6: Determine cophenetic correlation coefficient
c = cophenet(Z,Y)

Step 7: Construct the Dendrogram
dendrogram(Z)

Output:
c = 0.6307

3.11 Method-11: Cosine and complete

Step 1: Define the Matrix
X = [4 4;1 2;4 4;4 4;4 4;4 3;5 5;3 3;4 4;3 3;4 4;3 2;
 2 2;2 2;5 5;2 3;4 4;3 2;5 5;3 3;2 2;5 5;4 4;4 4;3 3]

Step 2: Find the Distance Information
Y = pdist(X)

Step 3: Generate the Squareform
squareform(Y)

Step 4: Find the Pairwise Distance
Y = pdist(X,'cosine')

Step 5: Find the Cluster Linkage
Z = linkage(Y,'complete')

Step 6: Determine cophenetic correlation coefficient
c = cophenet(Z,Y)

Step 7: Construct the Dendrogram
dendrogram(Z)

Output:
c = 0.6007

3.12 Method-12: correlation and average

Step 1: Define the Matrix
X = [4 4;1 2;4 4;4 4;4 4;4 3;5 5;3 3;4 4;3 3;4 4;3 2;
    2 2;2 2;5 5;2 3;4 4;3 2;5 5;3 3;2 2;5 5;4 4;4 4;3 3]

Step 2: Find the Distance Information
Y = pdist(X)

Step 3: Generate the Squareform
squareform(Y)

Step 4: Find the Pairwise Distance
Y = pdist(X,'correlation')

Step 5: Find the Cluster Linkage
Z = linkage(Y,'average')

Step 6: Determine cophenetic correlation coefficient
c = cophenet(Z,Y)

Step 7: Construct the Dendrogram
dendrogram(Z)

Output:
c = Nan

3.13 Method-13: Spearman and average

Step 1: Define the Matrix
X = [4 4;1 2;4 4;4 4;4 4;4 3;5 5;3 3;4 4;3 3;4 4;3 2;
　　2 2;2 2;5 5;2 3;4 4;3 2;5 5;3 3;2 2;5 5;4 4;4 4;3 3]

Step 2: Find the Distance Information
Y = pdist(X)

Step 3: Generate the Squareform
squareform(Y)

Step 4: Find the Pairwise Distance
Y = pdist(X,'spearman')

Step 5: Find the Cluster Linkage
Z = linkage(Y,'average')

Step 6: Determine cophenetic correlation coefficient
c = cophenet(Z,Y)

Step 7: Construct the Dendrogram
dendrogram(Z)

Output:
c = Nan

3.14 Method-14: Hamming and average

Step 1: Define the Matrix
X = [4 4;1 2;4 4;4 4;4 4;4 3;5 5;3 3;4 4;3 3;4 4;3 2;
2 2;2 2;5 5;2 3;4 4;3 2;5 5;3 3;2 2;5 5;4 4;4 4;3 3]

Step 2: Find the Distance Information
Y = pdist(X)

Step 3: Generate the Squareform
squareform(Y)

Step 4: Find the Pairwise Distance
Y = pdist(X,'hamming')

Step 5: Find the Cluster Linkage
Z = linkage(Y,'average')

Step 6: Determine cophenetic correlation coefficient
c = cophenet(Z,Y)

Step 7: Construct the Dendrogram
dendrogram(Z)

Output:
c = 0.8644

3.15 Method-15: Jaccard and average

Step 1: Define the Matrix
X = [4 4;1 2;4 4;4 4;4 4;4 3;5 5;3 3;4 4;3 3;4 4;3 2;
     2 2;2 2;5 5;2 3;4 4;3 2;5 5;3 3;2 2;5 5;4 4;4 4;3 3]

Step 2: Find the Distance Information
Y = pdist(X)

Step 3: Generate the Squareform
squareform(Y)

Step 4: Find the Pairwise Distance
Y = pdist(X,'jaccard')

Step 5: Find the Cluster Linkage
Z = linkage(Y,'average')

Step 6: Determine cophenetic correlation coefficient
c = cophenet(Z,Y)

Step 7: Construct the Dendrogram
dendrogram(Z)

Output:
c = 0.8644

3.16 Method-16: Seuclidean and centroid

Step 1: Define the Matrix
X = [4 4;1 2;4 4;4 4;4 4;4 3;5 5;3 3;4 4;3 3;4 4;3 2;
 2 2;2 2;5 5;2 3;4 4;3 2;5 5;3 3;2 2;5 5;4 4;4 4;3 3]

Step 2: Find the Distance Information
Y = pdist(X)

Step 3: Generate the Squareform
squareform(Y)

Step 4: Find the Pairwise Distance
Y = pdist(X,'seuclidean')

Step 5: Find the Cluster Linkage
Z = linkage(Y,'centroid')

Step 6: Determine cophenetic correlation coefficient
c = cophenet(Z,Y)

Step 7: Construct the Dendrogram
dendrogram(Z)

Output:
c = 0.8150

3.17 Method-17: Cityblock and centroid

Step 1: Define the Matrix
X = [4 4;1 2;4 4;4 4;4 4;4 3;5 5;3 3;4 4;3 3;4 4;3 2;
 2 2;2 2;5 5;2 3;4 4;3 2;5 5;3 3;2 2;5 5;4 4;4 4;3 3]

Step 2: Find the Distance Information
Y = pdist(X)

Step 3: Generate the Squareform
squareform(Y)

Step 4: Find the Pairwise Distance
Y = pdist(X,'cityblock')

Step 5: Find the Cluster Linkage
Z = linkage(Y,'centroid')

Step 6: Determine cophenetic correlation coefficient
c = cophenet(Z,Y)

Step 7: Construct the Dendrogram
dendrogram(Z)

Output:
c = 0.7790

3.18 Method-18: Minkowski and centroid

Step 1: Define the Matrix
X = [4 4;1 2;4 4;4 4;4 4;4 3;5 5;3 3;4 4;3 3;4 4;3 2;
 2 2;2 2;5 5;2 3;4 4;3 2;5 5;3 3;2 2;5 5;4 4;4 4;3 3]

Step 2: Find the Distance Information
Y = pdist(X)

Step 3: Generate the Squareform
squareform(Y)

Step 4: Find the Pairwise Distance
Y = pdist(X,'minkowski')

Step 5: Find the Cluster Linkage
Z = linkage(Y,'centroid')

Step 6: Determine cophenetic correlation coefficient
c = cophenet(Z,Y)

Step 7: Construct the Dendrogram
dendrogram(Z)

Output:
c = 0.7892

3.19 Method-19: Chebychew and centroid

Step 1: Define the Matrix
X = [4 4;1 2;4 4;4 4;4 4;4 3;5 5;3 3;4 4;3 3;4 4;3 2;
    2 2;2 2;5 5;2 3;4 4;3 2;5 5;3 3;2 2;5 5;4 4;4 4;3 3]

Step 2: Find the Distance Information
Y = pdist(X)

Step 3: Generate the Squareform
squareform(Y)

Step 4: Find the Pairwise Distance
Y = pdist(X,'chebychev')

Step 5: Find the Cluster Linkage
Z = linkage(Y,'centroid')

Step 6: Determine cophenetic correlation coefficient
c = cophenet(Z,Y)

Step 7: Construct the Dendrogram
dendrogram(Z)

Output:
c = 0.7805

3.20 Method-20: Mahalanobis and centroid

Step 1: Define the Matrix
X = [4 4;1 2;4 4;4 4;4 4;4 3;5 5;3 3;4 4;3 3;4 4;3 2;
     2 2;2 2;5 5;2 3;4 4;3 2;5 5;3 3;2 2;5 5;4 4;4 4;3 3]

Step 2: Find the Distance Information
Y = pdist(X)

Step 3: Generate the Squareform
squareform(Y)

Step 4: Find the Pairwise Distance
Y = pdist(X,'mahalanobis')

Step 5: Find the Cluster Linkage
Z = linkage(Y,'centroid')

Step 6: Determine cophenetic correlation coefficient
c = cophenet(Z,Y)

Step 7: Construct the Dendrogram
dendrogram(Z)

Output:
c = 0.7717

3.21 Method-21: Cosine and centroid

Step 1: Define the Matrix
X = [4 4;1 2;4 4;4 4;4 4;4 3;5 5;3 3;4 4;3 3;4 4;3 2;
    2 2;2 2;5 5;2 3;4 4;3 2;5 5;3 3;2 2;5 5;4 4;4 4;3 3]

Step 2: Find the Distance Information
Y = pdist(X)

Step 3: Generate the Squareform
squareform(Y)

Step 4: Find the Pairwise Distance
Y = pdist(X,'cosine')

Step 5: Find the Cluster Linkage
Z = linkage(Y,'centroid')

Step 6: Determine cophenetic correlation coefficient
c = cophenet(Z,Y)

Step 7: Construct the Dendrogram
dendrogram(Z)

Output:
c = 0.6282

3.22 Method-22: Correlation and centroid

Step 1: Define the Matrix
X = [4 4;1 2;4 4;4 4;4 4;4 3;5 5;3 3;4 4;3 3;4 4;3 2;
    2 2;2 2;5 5;2 3;4 4;3 2;5 5;3 3;2 2;5 5;4 4;4 4;3 3]

Step 2: Find the Distance Information
Y = pdist(X)

Step 3: Generate the Squareform
squareform(Y)

Step 4: Find the Pairwise Distance
Y = pdist(X,'correlation')

Step 5: Find the Cluster Linkage
Z = linkage(Y,'centroid')

Step 6: Determine cophenetic correlation coefficient
c = cophenet(Z,Y)

Step 7: Construct the Dendrogram
dendrogram(Z)

Output:
c = Nan

3.23 Method-23: Spearman and centroid

Step 1: Define the Matrix
X = [4 4;1 2;4 4;4 4;4 4;4 3;5 5;3 3;4 4;3 3;4 4;3 2;
 2 2;2 2;5 5;2 3;4 4;3 2;5 5;3 3;2 2;5 5;4 4;4 4;3 3]

Step 2: Find the Distance Information
Y = pdist(X)

Step 3: Generate the Squareform
squareform(Y)

Step 4: Find the Pairwise Distance
Y = pdist(X,'spearman')

Step 5: Find the Cluster Linkage
Z = linkage(Y,'centroid')

Step 6: Determine cophenetic correlation coefficient
c = cophenet(Z,Y)

Step 7: Construct the Dendrogram
dendrogram(Z)

Output:
c = Nan

3.24 Method-24: Hamming and centroid

Step 1: Define the Matrix
X = [4 4;1 2;4 4;4 4;4 4;4 3;5 5;3 3;4 4;3 3;4 4;3 2;
    2 2;2 2;5 5;2 3;4 4;3 2;5 5;3 3;2 2;5 5;4 4;4 4;3 3]

Step 2: Find the Distance Information
Y = pdist(X)

Step 3: Generate the Squareform
squareform(Y)

Step 4: Find the Pairwise Distance
Y = pdist(X,'hamming')

Step 5: Find the Cluster Linkage
Z = linkage(Y,'centroid')

Step 6: Determine cophenetic correlation coefficient
c = cophenet(Z,Y)

Step 7: Construct the Dendrogram
dendrogram(Z)

Output:
c = 0.8474

3.25 Method-25 Jaccard and centroid

Step 1: Define the Matrix
X = [4 4;1 2;4 4;4 4;4 4;4 3;5 5;3 3;4 4;3 3;4 4;3 2;
    2 2;2 2;5 5;2 3;4 4;3 2;5 5;3 3;2 2;5 5;4 4;4 4;3 3]

Step 2: Find the Distance Information
Y = pdist(X)

Step 3: Generate the Squareform
squareform(Y)

Step 4: Find the Pairwise Distance
Y = pdist(X,'jaccard')

Step 5: Find the Cluster Linkage
Z = linkage(Y,'centroid')

Step 6: Determine cophenetic correlation coefficient
c = cophenet(Z,Y)

Step 7: Construct the Dendrogram
dendrogram(Z)

Output:
c = 0.8477

3.26 Method-26: Euclidean and complete

Step 1: Define the Matrix
X = [4 4;1 2;4 4;4 4;4 4;4 3;5 5;3 3;4 4;3 3;4 4;3 2;
　　2 2;2 2;5 5;2 3;4 4;3 2;5 5;3 3;2 2;5 5;4 4;4 4;3 3]

Step 2: Find the Distance Information
Y = pdist(X)

Step 3: Generate the Squareform
squareform(Y)

Step 4: Find the Pairwise Distance
Y = pdist(X,'euclidean')

Step 5: Find the Cluster Linkage
Z = linkage(Y,'complete')

Step 6: Determine cophenetic correlation coefficient
c = cophenet(Z,Y)

Step 7: Construct the Dendrogram
dendrogram(Z)

Output:
c = 0.8087

3.27 Method-27: Seuclidean and complete

Step 1: Define the Matrix
X = [4 4;1 2;4 4;4 4;4 4;4 3;5 5;3 3;4 4;3 3;4 4;3 2;
2 2;2 2;5 5;2 3;4 4;3 2;5 5;3 3;2 2;5 5;4 4;4 4;3 3]

Step 2: Find the Distance Information
Y = pdist(X)

Step 3: Generate the Squareform
squareform(Y)

Step 4: Find the Pairwise Distance
Y = pdist(X,'seuclidean')

Step 5: Find the Cluster Linkage
Z = linkage(Y,'complete')

Step 6: Determine cophenetic correlation coefficient
c = cophenet(Z,Y)

Step 7: Construct the Dendrogram
dendrogram(Z)

Output:
c = 0.7010

3.28 Method- 28: Cityblock and complete

Step 1: Define the Matrix
X = [4 4;1 2;4 4;4 4;4 4;4 3;5 5;3 3;4 4;3 3;4 4;3 2;
     2 2;2 2;5 5;2 3;4 4;3 2;5 5;3 3;2 2;5 5;4 4;4 4;3 3]

Step 2: Find the Distance Information
Y = pdist(X)

Step 3: Generate the Squareform
squareform(Y)

Step 4: Find the Pairwise Distance
Y = pdist(X,'cityblock')

Step 5: Find the Cluster Linkage
Z = linkage(Y,'complete')

Step 6: Determine cophenetic correlation coefficient
c = cophenet(Z,Y)

Step 7: Construct the Dendrogram
dendrogram(Z)

Output:
c = 0.7590

3.29 Method-29: Minkowski and complete

Step 1: Define the Matrix
X = [4 4;1 2;4 4;4 4;4 4;4 3;5 5;3 3;4 4;3 3;4 4;3 2;
   2 2;2 2;5 5;2 3;4 4;3 2;5 5;3 3;2 2;5 5;4 4;4 4;3 3]

Step 2: Find the Distance Information
Y = pdist(X)

Step 3: Generate the Squareform
squareform(Y)

Step 4: Find the Pairwise Distance
Y = pdist(X,'minkowski')

Step 5: Find the Cluster Linkage
Z = linkage(Y,'complete')

Step 6: Determine cophenetic correlation coefficient
c = cophenet(Z,Y)

Step 7: Construct the Dendrogram
dendrogram(Z)

Output:
c = 0.7074

3.30 Method-30: Chebychev and complete

Step 1: Define the Matrix
X = [4 4;1 2;4 4;4 4;4 4;4 3;5 5;3 3;4 4;3 3;4 4;3 2;
   2 2;2 2;5 5;2 3;4 4;3 2;5 5;3 3;2 2;5 5;4 4;4 4;3 3]

Step 2: Find the Distance Information
Y = pdist(X)

Step 3: Generate the Squareform
squareform(Y)

Step 4: Find the Pairwise Distance
Y = pdist(X,'chebychev')

Step 5: Find the Cluster Linkage
Z = linkage(Y,'complete')

Step 6: Determine cophenetic correlation coefficient
c = cophenet(Z,Y)

Step 7: Construct the Dendrogram
dendrogram(Z)

Output:
c = 0.7466

Data Processing of Category C Employees

CHAPTER - IV

CHAPTER 4
DATA PROCESSING OF CATEGORY C EMPLOYEES

4.1 Method-1: 'euclidean' and 'average'

Step 1: Define the Matrix
X = [4 4;1 2;4 4;4 4;4 4;3;5 5;3 3;4 4;3 3;4 4;3 2;
2 2;2 2;5 5;2 3;4 4;3 2;5 5;3 3;2 2;5 5;4 4;4 4;3 3]

Step 2: Find the Distance Information
Y = pdist(X)

Step 3: Generate the Squareform
squareform(Y)

Step 4: Find the Pairwise Distance
Y = pdist(X,'euclidean')

Step 5: Find the Cluster Linkage
Z = linkage(Y,'average')

Step 6: Determine cophenetic correlation coefficient
c = cophenet(Z,Y)

Step 7: Construct the Dendrogram
dendrogram(Z)

Output:
c = 0.8154

4.2 Method-2: 'euclidean' and 'centroid'

Step 1: Define the Matrix
X = [4 4;1 2;4 4;4 4;4 4;4 3;5 5;3 3;4 4;3 3;4 4;3 2;
    2 2;2 2;5 5;2 3;4 4;3 2;5 5;3 3;2 2;5 5;4 4;4 4;3 3]

Step 2: Find the Distance Information
Y = pdist(X)

Step 3: Generate the Squareform
squareform(Y)

Step 4: Find the Pairwise Distance
Y = pdist(X,'euclidean')

Step 5: Find the Cluster Linkage
Z = linkage(Y,'centroid')

Step 6: Determine cophenetic correlation coefficient
c = cophenet(Z,Y)

Step 7: Construct the Dendrogram
dendrogram(Z)

Output:
c = 0.8150

4.3 Method-3: 'euclidean' and 'complete'

Step 1: Define the Matrix
X = [4 4;1 2;4 4;4 4;4 4;4 3;5 5;3 3;4 4;3 3;4 4;3 2;
     2 2;2 2;5 5;2 3;4 4;3 2;5 5;3 3;2 2;5 5;4 4;4 4;3 3]

Step 2: Find the Distance Information
Y = pdist(X)

Step 3: Generate the Squareform
squareform(Y)

Step 4: Find the Pairwise Distance
Y = pdist(X,'euclidean')

Step 5: Find the Cluster Linkage
Z = linkage(Y,'complete')

Step 6: Determine cophenetic correlation coefficient
c = cophenet(Z,Y)

Step 7: Construct the Dendrogram
dendrogram(Z)

Output:
c = 0.8087

4.4 Method-4: 'euclidean' and 'median'

Step 1: Define the Matrix
X = [4 4;1 2;4 4;4 4;4 4;4 3;5 5;3 3;4 4;3 3;4 4;3 2;
　　2 2;2 2;5 5;2 3;4 4;3 2;5 5;3 3;2 2;5 5;4 4;4 4;3 3]

Step 2: Find the Distance Information
Y = pdist(X)

Step 3: Generate the Squareform
squareform(Y)

Step 4: Find the Pairwise Distance
Y = pdist(X,'euclidean')

Step 5: Find the Cluster Linkage
Z = linkage(Y,'median')

Step 6: Determine cophenetic correlation coefficient
c = cophenet(Z,Y)

Step 7: Construct the Dendrogram
dendrogram(Z)

Output:
c = 0.7075

4.5 Method-5: Euclidean and Single

Step 1: Define the Matrix
X = [4 4;1 2;4 4;4 4;4 4;4 3;5 5;3 3;4 4;3 3;4 4;3 2;
    2 2;2 2;5 5;2 3;4 4;3 2;5 5;3 3;2 2;5 5;4 4;4 4;3 3]

Step 2: Find the Distance Information
Y = pdist(X)

Step 3: Generate the Squareform
squareform(Y)

Step 4: Find the Pairwise Distance
Y = pdist(X,'euclidean')

Step 5: Find the Cluster Linkage
Z = linkage(Y,'single')

Step 6: Determine cophenetic correlation coefficient
c = cophenet(Z,Y)

Step 7: Construct the Dendrogram
dendrogram(Z)

Output:
c = 0.7075

4.6 Method-6: Euclidean and Ward

Step 1: Define the Matrix
X = [4 4;1 2;4 4;4 4;4 4;4 3;5 5;3 3;4 4;3 3;4 4;3 2;
2 2;2 2;5 5;2 3;4 4;3 2;5 5;3 3;2 2;5 5;4 4;4 4;3 3]

Step 2: Find the Distance Information
Y = pdist(X)

Step 3: Generate the Squareform
squareform(Y)

Step 4: Find the Pairwise Distance
Y = pdist(X,'euclidean')

Step 5: Find the Cluster Linkage
Z = linkage(Y,'ward')

Step 6: Determine cophenetic correlation coefficient
c = cophenet(Z,Y)

Step 7: Construct the Dendrogram
dendrogram(Z)

Output:
c = 0.7676

4.7 Method-7: Euclidean and weighted

Step 1: Define the Matrix
X = [4 4;1 2;4 4;4 4;4 4;4 3;5 5;3 3;4 4;3 3;4 4;3 2;
2 2;2 2;5 5;2 3;4 4;3 2;5 5;3 3;2 2;5 5;4 4;4 4;3 3]

Step 2: Find the Distance Information
Y = pdist(X)

Step 3: Generate the Squareform
squareform(Y)

Step 4: Find the Pairwise Distance
Y = pdist(X,'euclidean')

Step 5: Find the Cluster Linkage
Z = linkage(Y,'weighted')

Step 6: Determine cophenetic correlation coefficient
c = cophenet(Z,Y)

Step 7: Construct the Dendrogram
dendrogram(Z)

Output:
c = 0.7969

4.8 Method-8: Chebychev and average

Step 1: Define the Matrix
X = [4 4;1 2;4 4;4 4;4 4;4 3;5 5;3 3;4 4;3 3;4 4;3 2;
    2 2;2 2;5 5;2 3;4 4;3 2;5 5;3 3;2 2;5 5;4 4;4 4;3 3]

Step 2: Find the Distance Information
Y = pdist(X)

Step 3: Generate the Squareform
squareform(Y)

Step 4: Find the Pairwise Distance
Y = pdist(X,'chebychev')

Step 5: Find the Cluster Linkage
Z = linkage(Y,'average')

Step 6: Determine cophenetic correlation coefficient
c = cophenet(Z,Y)

Step 7: Construct the Dendrogram
dendrogram(Z)

Output:
c = 0.8154

4.9 Method-9: Mahalanobis and average

Step 1: Define the Matrix
X = [4 4;1 2;4 4;4 4;4 4;4 3;5 5;3 3;4 4;3 3;4 4;3 2;
2 2;2 2;5 5;2 3;4 4;3 2;5 5;3 3;2 2;5 5;4 4;4 4;3 3]

Step 2: Find the Distance Information
Y = pdist(X)

Step 3: Generate the Squareform
squareform(Y)

Step 4: Find the Pairwise Distance
Y = pdist(X,'mahalanobis')

Step 5: Find the Cluster Linkage
Z = linkage(Y,'average')

Step 6: Determine cophenetic correlation coefficient
c = cophenet(Z,Y)

Step 7: Construct the Dendrogram
dendrogram(Z)

Output:
c = 0.8966

4.10 Method-10: Cosine and average

Step 1: Define the Matrix
X = [4 4;1 2;4 4;4 4;4 4;4 3;5 5;3 3;4 4;3 3;4 4;3 2;
    2 2;2 2;5 5;2 3;4 4;3 2;5 5;3 3;2 2;5 5;4 4;4 4;3 3]

Step 2: Find the Distance Information
Y = pdist(X)

Step 3: Generate the Squareform
squareform(Y)

Step 4: Find the Pairwise Distance
Y = pdist(X,'cosine')

Step 5: Find the Cluster Linkage
Z = linkage(Y,'average')

Step 6: Determine cophenetic correlation coefficient
c = cophenet(Z,Y)

Step 7: Construct the Dendrogram
dendrogram(Z)

Output:
c = 0.8915

4.11 Method-11: Cityblock and average

Step 1: Define the Matrix
X = [4 4;1 2;4 4;4 4;4 4;4 3;5 5;3 3;4 4;3 3;4 4;3 2;
2 2;2 2;5 5;2 3;4 4;3 2;5 5;3 3;2 2;5 5;4 4;4 4;3 3]

Step 2: Find the Distance Information
Y = pdist(X)

Step 3: Generate the Squareform
squareform(Y)

Step 4: Find the Pairwise Distance
Y = pdist(X,'cityblock')

Step 5: Find the Cluster Linkage
Z = linkage(Y,'average')

Step 6: Determine cophenetic correlation coefficient
c = cophenet(Z,Y)

Step 7: Construct the Dendrogram
dendrogram(Z)

Output:
c = 0.8169

4.12 Method-12: Seuclidean and single

Step 1: Define the Matrix
X = [4 4;1 2;4 4;4 4;4 4;4 3;5 5;3 3;4 4;3 3;4 4;3 2;
    2 2;2 2;5 5;2 3;4 4;3 2;5 5;3 3;2 2;5 5;4 4;4 4;3 3]

Step 2: Find the Distance Information
Y = pdist(X)

Step 3: Generate the Squareform
squareform(Y)

Step 4: Find the Pairwise Distance
Y = pdist(X,'seuclidean')

Step 5: Find the Cluster Linkage
Z = linkage(Y,'single')

Step 6: Determine cophenetic correlation coefficient
c = cophenet(Z,Y)

Step 7: Construct the Dendrogram
dendrogram(Z)

Output:
c = 0.7066

4.13 Method-13: cityblock and single

Step 1: Define the Matrix
X = [4 4;1 2;4 4;4 4;4 4;4 3;5 5;3 3;4 4;3 3;4 4;3 2;
    2 2;2 2;5 5;2 3;4 4;3 2;5 5;3 3;2 2;5 5;4 4;4 4;3 3]

Step 2: Find the Distance Information
Y = pdist(X)

Step 3: Generate the Squareform
squareform(Y)

Step 4: Find the Pairwise Distance
Y = pdist(X,'cityblock')

Step 5: Find the Cluster Linkage
Z = linkage(Y,'single')

Step 6: Determine cophenetic correlation coefficient
c = cophenet(Z,Y)

Step 7: Construct the Dendrogram
dendrogram(Z)

Output:
c = 0.7510

4.14 Method-14: Hamming and average

Step 1: Define the Matrix
X = [4 4;1 2;4 4;4 4;4 4;4 3;5 5;3 3;4 4;3 3;4 4;3 2;
    2 2;2 2;5 5;2 3;4 4;3 2;5 5;3 3;2 2;5 5;4 4;4 4;3 3]

Step 2: Find the Distance Information
Y = pdist(X)

Step 3: Generate the Squareform
squareform(Y)

Step 4: Find the Pairwise Distance
Y = pdist(X,'hamming')

Step 5: Find the Cluster Linkage
Z = linkage(Y,'average')

Step 6: Determine cophenetic correlation coefficient
c = cophenet(Z,Y)

Step 7: Construct the Dendrogram
dendrogram(Z)

Output:
c = 0.9602

4.15 Method-15: Jaccard and average

Step 1: Define the Matrix
X = [4 4;1 2;4 4;4 4;4 4;4 3;5 5;3 3;4 4;3 3;4 4;3 2;
     2 2;2 2;5 5;2 3;4 4;3 2;5 5;3 3;2 2;5 5;4 4;4 4;3 3]

Step 2: Find the Distance Information
Y = pdist(X)

Step 3: Generate the Squareform
squareform(Y)

Step 4: Find the Pairwise Distance
Y = pdist(X,'jaccard')

Step 5: Find the Cluster Linkage
Z = linkage(Y,'average')

Step 6: Determine cophenetic correlation coefficient
c = cophenet(Z,Y)

Step 7: Construct the Dendrogram
dendrogram(Z)

Output:
c = 0.9602

4.16 Method-16: seuclidean and centroid

Step 1: Define the Matrix
X = [4 4;1 2;4 4;4 4;4 4;4 3;5 5;3 3;4 4;3 3;4 4;3 2;
 2 2;2 2;5 5;2 3;4 4;3 2;5 5;3 3;2 2;5 5;4 4;4 4;3 3]

Step 2: Find the Distance Information
Y = pdist(X)

Step 3: Generate the Squareform
squareform(Y)

Step 4: Find the Pairwise Distance
Y = pdist(X,'seuclidean')

Step 5: Find the Cluster Linkage
Z = linkage(Y,'centroid')

Step 6: Determine cophenetic correlation coefficient
c = cophenet(Z,Y)

Step 7: Construct the Dendrogram
dendrogram(Z)

Output:
c =0.8150

4.17 Method-17: cityblock and centroid

Step 1: Define the Matrix
X = [4 4;1 2;4 4;4 4;4 4;4 3;5 5;3 3;4 4;3 3;4 4;3 2;
    2 2;2 2;5 5;2 3;4 4;3 2;5 5;3 3;2 2;5 5;4 4;4 4;3 3]

Step 2: Find the Distance Information
Y = pdist(X)

Step 3: Generate the Squareform
squareform(Y)

Step 4: Find the Pairwise Distance
Y = pdist(X,'cityblock')

Step 5: Find the Cluster Linkage
Z = linkage(Y,'centroid')

Step 6: Determine cophenetic correlation coefficient
c = cophenet(Z,Y)

Step 7: Construct the Dendrogram
dendrogram(Z)

Output:
c = 0.8169

4.18 Method-18: Minkowski and centroid

Step 1: Define the Matrix
X = [4 4;1 2;4 4;4 4;4 4;4 3;5 5;3 3;4 4;3 3;4 4;3 2;
    2 2;2 2;5 5;2 3;4 4;3 2;5 5;3 3;2 2;5 5;4 4;4 4;3 3]

Step 2: Find the Distance Information
Y = pdist(X)

Step 3: Generate the Squareform
squareform(Y)

Step 4: Find the Pairwise Distance
Y = pdist(X,'minkowski')

Step 5: Find the Cluster Linkage
Z = linkage(Y,'centroid')

Step 6: Determine cophenetic correlation coefficient
c = cophenet(Z,Y)

Step 7: Construct the Dendrogram
dendrogram(Z)

Output:
c = 0.8150

4.19 Method-19: chebychev and centroid

Step 1: Define the Matrix
X = [4 4;1 2;4 4;4 4;4 4;3 5 5;3 3;4 4;3 3;4 4;3 2;
    2 2;2 2;5 5;2 3;4 4;3 2;5 5;3 3;2 2;5 5;4 4;4 4;3 3]

Step 2: Find the Distance Information
Y = pdist(X)

Step 3: Generate the Squareform
squareform(Y)

Step 4: Find the Pairwise Distance
Y = pdist(X,'chebychev')

Step 5: Find the Cluster Linkage
Z = linkage(Y,'centroid')

Step 6: Determine cophenetic correlation coefficient
c = cophenet(Z,Y)

Step 7: Construct the Dendrogram
dendrogram(Z)

Output:
c = 0.8143

4.20 Method-20: Mahalanobis and centroid

Step 1: Define the Matrix
X = [4 4;1 2;4 4;4 4;4 4;4 3;5 5;3 3;4 4;3 3;4 4;3 2;
    2 2;2 2;5 5;2 3;4 4;3 2;5 5;3 3;2 2;5 5;4 4;4 4;3 3]

Step 2: Find the Distance Information
Y = pdist(X)

Step 3: Generate the Squareform
squareform(Y)

Step 4: Find the Pairwise Distance
Y = pdist(X,'mahalanobis')

Step 5: Find the Cluster Linkage
Z = linkage(Y,'centroid')

Step 6: Determine cophenetic correlation coefficient
c = cophenet(Z,Y)

Step 7: Construct the Dendrogram
dendrogram(Z)

Output:
c = 0.8959

4.21 Method-21: Cosine and centroid

Step 1: Define the Matrix
X = [4 4;1 2;4 4;4 4;4 4;3 5;5 3;3;4 4;3 3;4 4;3 2;
    2 2;2 2;5 5;2 3;4 4;3 2;5 5;3 3;2 2;5 5;4 4;4 4;3 3]

Step 2: Find the Distance Information
Y = pdist(X)

Step 3: Generate the Squareform
squareform(Y)

Step 4: Find the Pairwise Distance
Y = pdist(X,'cosine')

Step 5: Find the Cluster Linkage
Z = linkage(Y,'centroid')

Step 6: Determine cophenetic correlation coefficient
c = cophenet(Z,Y)

Step 7: Construct the Dendrogram
dendrogram(Z)

Output:
c = 0.8902

4.22 Method-22: Minkowski and single

Step 1: Define the Matrix
X = [4 4;1 2;4 4;4 4;4 4;4 3;5 5;3 3;4 4;3 3;4 4;3 2;
      2 2;2 2;5 5;2 3;4 4;3 2;5 5;3 3;2 2;5 5;4 4;4 4;3 3]

Step 2: Find the Distance Information
Y = pdist(X)

Step 3: Generate the Squareform
squareform(Y)

Step 4: Find the Pairwise Distance
Y = pdist(X,'minkowski')

Step 5: Find the Cluster Linkage
Z = linkage(Y,'single')

Step 6: Determine cophenetic correlation coefficient
c = cophenet(Z,Y)

Step 7: Construct the Dendrogram
dendrogram(Z)

Output:
c = 0.7075

4.23 Method-23: Mahalanobis and single

Step 1: Define the Matrix
X = [4 4;1 2;4 4;4 4;4 4;4 3;5 5;3 3;4 4;3 3;4 4;3 2;
   2 2;2 2;5 5;2 3;4 4;3 2;5 5;3 3;2 2;5 5;4 4;4 4;3 3]

Step 2: Find the Distance Information
Y = pdist(X)

Step 3: Generate the Squareform
squareform(Y)

Step 4: Find the Pairwise Distance
Y = pdist(X,'mahalanobis')

Step 5: Find the Cluster Linkage
Z = linkage(Y,'single')

Step 6: Determine cophenetic correlation coefficient
c = cophenet(Z,Y)

Step 7: Construct the Dendrogram
dendrogram(Z)

Output:
c = 0.8025

4.24 Method-24: Hamming and Centroid

Step 1: Define the Matrix
X = [4 4;1 2;4 4;4 4;4 4;4 3;5 5;3 3;4 4;3 3;4 4;3 2;
      2 2;2 2;5 5;2 3;4 4;3 2;5 5;3 3;2 2;5 5;4 4;4 4;3 3]

Step 2: Find the Distance Information
Y = pdist(X)

Step 3: Generate the Squareform
squareform(Y)

Step 4: Find the Pairwise Distance
Y = pdist(X,'hamming')

Step 5: Find the Cluster Linkage
Z = linkage(Y,'centroid')

Step 6: Determine cophenetic correlation coefficient
c = cophenet(Z,Y)

Step 7: Construct the Dendrogram
dendrogram(Z)

Output:
c =0.9461

4.25 Method-25: Jaccard and centroid

Step 1: Define the Matrix
X = [4 4;1 2;4 4;4 4;4 4;4 3;5 5;3 3;4 4;3 3;4 4;3 2;
    2 2;2 2;5 5;2 3;4 4;3 2;5 5;3 3;2 2;5 5;4 4;4 4;3 3]

Step 2: Find the Distance Information
Y = pdist(X)

Step 3: Generate the Squareform
squareform(Y)

Step 4: Find the Pairwise Distance
Y = pdist(X,'jaccard')

Step 5: Find the Cluster Linkage
Z = linkage(Y,'centroid')

Step 6: Determine cophenetic correlation coefficient
c = cophenet(Z,Y)

Step 7: Construct the Dendrogram
dendrogram(Z)

Output:
c = 0.9461

4.26 Method-26: Seuclidean and complete

Step 1: Define the Matrix
X = [4 4;1 2;4 4;4 4;4 4;4 3;5 5;3 3;4 4;3 3;4 4;3 2;
    2 2;2 2;5 5;2 3;4 4;3 2;5 5;3 3;2 2;5 5;4 4;4 4;3 3]

Step 2: Find the Distance Information
Y = pdist(X)

Step 3: Generate the Squareform
squareform(Y)

Step 4: Find the Pairwise Distance
Y = pdist(X,'seuclidean')

Step 5: Find the Cluster Linkage
Z = linkage(Y,'complete')

Step 6: Determine cophenetic correlation coefficient
c = cophenet(Z,Y)

Step 7: Construct the Dendrogram
dendrogram(Z)

Output:
c = 0.8086

4.27 Method-27: cityblock and complete

Step 1: Define the Matrix
X = [4 4;1 2;4 4;4 4;4 4;4 3;5 5;3 3;4 4;3 3;4 4;3 2;
    2 2;2 2;5 5;2 3;4 4;3 2;5 5;3 3;2 2;5 5;4 4;4 4;3 3]

Step 2: Find the Distance Information
Y = pdist(X)

Step 3: Generate the Squareform
squareform(Y)

Step 4: Find the Pairwise Distance
Y = pdist(X,'cityblock')

Step 5: Find the Cluster Linkage
Z = linkage(Y,'complete')

Step 6: Determine cophenetic correlation coefficient
c = cophenet(Z,Y)

Step 7: Construct the Dendrogram
dendrogram(Z)

Output:
c = 0.8115

4.28 Method- 28: Minkowski and complete

Step 1: Define the Matrix
X = [4 4;1 2;4 4;4 4;4 4;4 3;5 5;3 3;4 4;3 3;4 4;3 2;
     2 2;2 2;5 5;2 3;4 4;3 2;5 5;3 3;2 2;5 5;4 4;4 4;3 3]

Step 2: Find the Distance Information
Y = pdist(X)

Step 3: Generate the Squareform
squareform(Y)

Step 4: Find the Pairwise Distance
Y = pdist(X,'minkowski')

Step 5: Find the Cluster Linkage
Z = linkage(Y,'complete')

Step 6: Determine cophenetic correlation coefficient
c = cophenet(Z,Y)

Step 7: Construct the Dendrogram
dendrogram(Z)

Output:
c = 0.8087

4.29 Method-29: chebychev and complete

Step 1: Define the Matrix
X = [4 4;1 2;4 4;4 4;4 4;4 3;5 5;3 3;4 4;3 3;4 4;3 2;
2 2;2 2;5 5;2 3;4 4;3 2;5 5;3 3;2 2;5 5;4 4;4 4;3 3]

Step 2: Find the Distance Information
Y = pdist(X)

Step 3: Generate the Squareform
squareform(Y)

Step 4: Find the Pairwise Distance
Y = pdist(X,'chebychev')

Step 5: Find the Cluster Linkage
Z = linkage(Y,'complete')

Step 6: Determine cophenetic correlation coefficient
c = cophenet(Z,Y)

Step 7: Construct the Dendrogram
dendrogram(Z)

Output:
c =0.8072

4.30 Method-30: Mahalanobis and Complete

Step 1: Define the Matrix
X = [4 4;1 2;4 4;4 4;4 4;4 3;5 5;3 3;4 4;3 3;4 4;3 2;
2 2;2 2;5 5;2 3;4 4;3 2;5 5;3 3;2 2;5 5;4 4;4 4;3 3]

Step 2: Find the Distance Information
Y = pdist(X)

Step 3: Generate the Squareform
squareform(Y)

Step 4: Find the Pairwise Distance
Y = pdist(X,'mahalanobis')

Step 5: Find the Cluster Linkage
Z = linkage(Y,'complete')

Step 6: Determine cophenetic correlation coefficient
c = cophenet(Z,Y)

Step 7: Construct the Dendrogram
dendrogram(Z)

Output:
c = 0.8619

For Category-D Employees

CHAPTER - V

CHAPTER 5

FOR CATEGORY-D EMPLOYEES

5.1 Method-1: euclidean and single

Step 1: Score Matrix is generated

Step 2: Find the Distance Information
Y = pdist(X)

Step 3: Generate the Squareform
squareform(Y)

Step 4: Find the Pairwise Distance
Y = pdist(X,'euclidean')

Step 5: Find the Cluster Linkage
Z = linkage(Y,'single')

Step 6: Determine cophenetic correlation coefficient
c = cophenet(Z,Y)

Step 7: Construct the Dendrogram
dendrogram(Z)

Output:
c = 0.7938

5.2 Method-2: euclidean and complete

Step 1: Score Matrix is generated

Step 2: Find the Distance Information
Y = pdist(X)

Step 3: Generate the Squareform
squareform(Y)

Step 4: Find the Pairwise Distance
Y = pdist(X,'euclidean')

Step 5: Find the Cluster Linkage
Z = linkage(Y,'complete')

Step 6: Determine cophenetic correlation coefficient
c = cophenet(Z,Y)

Step 7: Construct the Dendrogram
dendrogram(Z)

Output:
c = 0.8085

5.3 Method-3: euclidean & average

Step 1: Score Matrix is generated

Step 2: Find the Distance Information
Y = pdist(X)

Step 3: Generate the Squareform
squareform(Y)

Step 4: Find the Pairwise Distance
Y = pdist(X,'euclidean')

Step 5: Find the Cluster Linkage
Z = linkage(Y,'average')

Step 6: Determine cophenetic correlation coefficient
c = cophenet(Z,Y)

Step 7: Construct the Dendrogram
dendrogram(Z)

Output:
c = 0.9188

5.4 Method-4: euclidean and centroid

Step 1: Score Matrix is generated

Step 2: Find the Distance Information
Y = pdist(X)

Step 3: Generate the Squareform
squareform(Y)

Step 4: Find the Pairwise Distance
Y = pdist(X,'euclidean')

Step 5: Find the Cluster Linkage
Z = linkage(Y,'centroid')

Step 6: Determine cophenetic correlation coefficient
c = cophenet(Z,Y)

Step 7: Construct the Dendrogram
dendrogram(Z)

Output:
c = 0.9172

5.5 Method-5: Seuclidean and single

Step 1: Score Matrix is generated

Step 2: Find the Distance Information
Y = pdist(X)

Step 3: Generate the Squareform
Squareform(Y)

Step 4: Find the Pairwise Distance
Y = pdist(X,'seuclidean')

Step 5: Find the Cluster Linkage
Z = linkage(Y,'single')

Step 6: Determine cophenetic correlation coefficient
c = cophenet(Z,Y)

Step 7: Construct the Dendrogram
dendrogram(Z)

Output:
c = 0.7958

5.6 Method-6: Seuclidean and complete

Step 1: Score Matrix is generated

Step 2: Find the Distance Information
Y = pdist(X)

Step 3: Generate the Squareform
squareform(Y)

Step 4: Find the Pairwise Distance
Y = pdist(X,'seuclidean')

Step 5: Find the Cluster Linkage
Z = linkage(Y,'complete')

Step 6: Determine cophenetic correlation coefficient
c = cophenet(Z,Y)

Step 7: Construct the Dendrogram
dendrogram(Z)

Output:
c = 0.8022

5.7 Method-7: Seulidean and average

Step 1: Score Matrix is generated

Step 2: Find the Distance Information
Y = pdist(X)

Step 3: Generate the Squareform
squareform(Y)

Step 4: Find the Pairwise Distance
Y = pdist(X,'seuclidean')

Step 5: Find the Cluster Linkage
Z = linkage(Y,'average')

Step 6: Determine cophenetic correlation coefficient
c = cophenet(Z,Y)

Step 7: Construct the Dendrogram
dendrogram(Z)

Output:
c = 0.9201

5.8 Method-8: Seluclidean and centroid

Step 1: Score Matrix is generated

Step 2: Find the Distance Information
Y = pdist(X)

Step 3: Generate the Squareform
squareform(Y)

Step 4: Find the Pairwise Distance
Y = pdist(X,'seuclidean')

Step 5: Find the Cluster Linkage
Z = linkage(Y,'centroid')

Step 6: Determine cophenetic correlation coefficient
c = cophenet(Z,Y)

Step 7: Construct the Dendrogram
dendrogram(Z)

Output:
c = 0.9187

5.9 Method-9: Cityblock and single

Step 1: Score Matrix is generated

Step 2: Find the Distance Information
Y = pdist(X)

Step 3: Generate the Squareform
squareform(Y)

Step 4: Find the Pairwise Distance
Y = pdist(X,'cityblock')

Step 5: Find the Cluster Linkage
Z = linkage(Y,'single')

Step 6: Determine cophenetic correlation coefficient
c = cophenet(Z,Y)

Step 7: Construct the Dendrogram
dendrogram(Z)

Output:
c = 0.8460

5.10 Method-10: Cityblock and complete

Step 1: Score Matrix is generated

Step 2: Find the Distance Information
Y = pdist(X)

Step 3: Generate the Squareform
squareform(Y)

Step 4: Find the Pairwise Distance
Y = pdist(X,'cityblock')

Step 5: Find the Cluster Linkage
Z = linkage(Y,'complete')

Step 6: Determine cophenetic correlation coefficient
c = cophenet(Z,Y)

Step 7: Construct the Dendrogram
dendrogram(Z)

Output:
c = 0.7804

5.11 Method-11: Cityblock and average

Step 1: Score Matrix is generated

Step 2: Find the Distance Information
Y = pdist(X)

Step 3: Generate the Squareform
squareform(Y)

Step 4: Find the Pairwise Distance
Y = pdist(X,'cityblock')

Step 5: Find the Cluster Linkage
Z = linkage(Y,'average')

Step 6: Determine cophenetic correlation coefficient
c = cophenet(Z,Y)

Step 7: Construct the Dendrogram
dendrogram(Z)

Output:
c = 0.9020

5.12 Method-12: Cityblock and centroid

Step 1: Score Matrix is generated

Step 2: Find the Distance Information
Y = pdist(X)

Step 3: Generate the Squareform
squareform(Y)

Step 4: Find the Pairwise Distance
Y = pdist(X,'cityblock')

Step 5: Find the Cluster Linkage
Z = linkage(Y,'centroid')

Step 6: Determine cophenetic correlation coefficient
c = cophenet(Z,Y)

Step 7: Construct the Dendrogram
dendrogram(Z)

Output:
c = 0.9019

5.13 Method-13: Minkowski and single

Step 1: Score Matrix is generated

Step 2: Find the Distance Information
Y = pdist(X)

Step 3: Generate the Squareform
squareform(Y)

Step 4: Find the Pairwise Distance
Y = pdist(X,'minkowski')

Step 5: Find the Cluster Linkage
Z = linkage(Y,'single')

Step 6: Determine cophenetic correlation coefficient
c = cophenet(Z,Y)

Step 7: Construct the Dendrogram
dendrogram(Z)

Output:
c = 0.7938

5.14 Method-14: Minkowski and complete

Step 1: Score Matrix is generated

Step 2: Find the Distance Information
Y = pdist(X)

Step 3: Generate the Squareform
squareform(Y)

Step 4: Find the Pairwise Distance
Y = pdist(X,'minkowski')

Step 5: Find the Cluster Linkage
Z = linkage(Y,'complete')

Step 6: Determine cophenetic correlation coefficient
c = cophenet(Z,Y)

Step 7: Construct the Dendrogram
dendrogram(Z)

Output:
c = 0.8085

5.15 Method-15: Minkowski and average

Step 1: Score Matrix is generated

Step 2: Find the Distance Information
Y = pdist(X)

Step 3: Generate the Squareform
squareform(Y)

Step 4: Find the Pairwise Distance
Y = pdist(X,'minkowski')

Step 5: Find the Cluster Linkage
Z = linkage(Y,'average')

Step 6: Determine cophenetic correlation coefficient
c = cophenet(Z,Y)

Step 7: Construct the Dendrogram
dendrogram(Z)

Output:
c = 0.9188

5.16 Method-16: Minkowski and centroid

Step 1: Score Matrix is generated

Step 2: Find the Distance Information
Y = pdist(X)

Step 3: Generate the Squareform
squareform(Y)

Step 4: Find the Pairwise Distance
Y = pdist(X,'minkowski')

Step 5: Find the Cluster Linkage
Z = linkage(Y,'centroid')

Step 6: Determine cophenetic correlation coefficient
c = cophenet(Z,Y)

Step 7: Construct the Dendrogram
dendrogram(Z)

Output:
c = 0.9172

5.17 Method-17: Chebychev and single

Step 1: Score Matrix is generated

Step 2: Find the Distance Information
Y = pdist(X)

Step 3: Generate the Squareform
squareform(Y)

Step 4: Find the Pairwise Distance
Y = pdist(X,'chebychev')

Step 5: Find the Cluster Linkage
Z = linkage(Y,'single')

Step 6: Determine cophenetic correlation coefficient
c = cophenet(Z,Y)

Step 7: Construct the Dendrogram
dendrogram(Z)

Output:
c = 0.6709

5.18 Method-18: Chebychev and complete

Step 1: Score Matrix is generated

Step 2: Find the Distance Information
Y = pdist(X)

Step 3: Generate the Squareform
squareform(Y)

Step 4: Find the Pairwise Distance
Y = pdist(X,'chebychev')

Step 5: Find the Cluster Linkage
Z = linkage(Y,'complete')

Step 6: Determine cophenetic correlation coefficient
c = cophenet(Z,Y)

Step 7: Construct the Dendrogram
dendrogram(Z)

Output:
c = 0.9159

5.19 Method-19: Chebychev and average

Step 1: Score Matrix is generated

Step 2: Find the Distance Information
Y = pdist(X)

Step 3: Generate the Squareform
squareform(Y)

Step 4: Find the Pairwise Distance
Y = pdist(X,'chebychev')

Step 5: Find the Cluster Linkage
Z = linkage(Y,'average')

Step 6: Determine cophenetic correlation coefficient
c = cophenet(Z,Y)

Step 7: Construct the Dendrogram
dendrogram(Z)

Output:
c = 0.9233

5.20 Method-20: Chebychev and centroid

Step 1: Score Matrix is generated

Step 2: Find the Distance Information
Y = pdist(X)

Step 3: Generate the Squareform
squareform(Y)

Step 4: Find the Pairwise Distance
Y = pdist(X,'chebychev')

Step 5: Find the Cluster Linkage
Z = linkage(Y,'centroid')

Step 6: Determine cophenetic correlation coefficient
c = cophenet(Z,Y)

Step 7: Construct the Dendrogram
dendrogram(Z)

Output:
c = 0.9202

5.21 Method-21: Mahalanobis and single

Step 1: Score Matrix is generated

Step 2: Find the Distance Information
Y = pdist(X)

Step 3: Generate the Squareform
squareform(Y)

Step 4: Find the Pairwise Distance
Y = pdist(X,'mahalanobis')

Step 5: Find the Cluster Linkage
Z = linkage(Y,'single')

Step 6: Determine cophenetic correlation coefficient
c = cophenet(Z,Y)

Step 7: Construct the Dendrogram
dendrogram(Z)

Output:
c = 0.7710

5.22 Method-22: Mahalanobis and complete

Step 1: Score Matrix is generated

Step 2: Find the Distance Information
Y = pdist(X)

Step 3: Generate the Squareform
squareform(Y)

Step 4: Find the Pairwise Distance
Y = pdist(X,'mahalanobis')

Step 5: Find the Cluster Linkage
Z = linkage(Y,'complete')

Step 6: Determine cophenetic correlation coefficient
c = cophenet(Z,Y)

Step 7: Construct the Dendrogram
dendrogram(Z)

Output:
c = 0.8587

5.23 Method-23: Mahalanobis and average

Step 1: Score Matrix is generated

Step 2: Find the Distance Information
Y = pdist(X)

Step 3: Generate the Squareform
squareform(Y)

Step 4: Find the Pairwise Distance
Y = pdist(X,'mahalanobis')

Step 5: Find the Cluster Linkage
Z = linkage(Y,'average')

Step 6: Determine cophenetic correlation coefficient
c = cophenet(Z,Y)

Step 7: Construct the Dendrogram
dendrogram(Z)

Output:
c = 0.8942

5.24 Method-24: Mahalanobis and centroid

Step 1: Score Matrix is generated

Step 2: Find the Distance Information
Y = pdist(X)

Step 3: Generate the Squareform
squareform(Y)

Step 4: Find the Pairwise Distance
Y = pdist(X,'mahalanobis')

Step 5: Find the Cluster Linkage
Z = linkage(Y,'centroid')

Step 6: Determine cophenetic correlation coefficient
c = cophenet(Z,Y)

Step 7: Construct the Dendrogram
dendrogram(Z)

Output:
c = 0.8933

5.25 Method-25: Cosine and single

Step 1: Score Matrix is generated

Step 2: Find the Distance Information
Y = pdist(X)

Step 3: Generate the Squareform
squareform(Y)

Step 4: Find the Pairwise Distance
Y = pdist(X,'cosine')

Step 5: Find the Cluster Linkage
Z = linkage(Y,'single')

Step 6: Determine cophenetic correlation coefficient
c = cophenet(Z,Y)

Step 7: Construct the Dendrogram
dendrogram(Z)

Output:
c = 0.7768

5.26 Method-26: Cosine and complete

Step 1: Score Matrix is generated

Step 2: Find the Distance Information
Y = pdist(X)

Step 3: Generate the Squareform
squareform(Y)

Step 4: Find the Pairwise Distance
Y = pdist(X,'cosine')

Step 5: Find the Cluster Linkage
Z = linkage(Y,'complete')

Step 6: Determine cophenetic correlation coefficient
c = cophenet(Z,Y)

Step 7: Construct the Dendrogram
dendrogram(Z)

Output:
c = 0.5936

5.27 Method-27: Cosine and average

Step 1: Score Matrix is generated

Step 2: Find the Distance Information
Y = pdist(X)

Step 3: Generate the Squareform
squareform(Y)

Step 4: Find the Pairwise Distance
Y = pdist(X,'cosine')

Step 5: Find the Cluster Linkage
Z = linkage(Y,'average')

Step 6: Determine cophenetic correlation coefficient
c = cophenet(Z,Y)

Step 7: Construct the Dendrogram
dendrogram(Z)

Output:
c = 0.7824

5.28 Method-28: Cosine and centroid

Step 1: Score Matrix is generated

Step 2: Find the Distance Information
Y = pdist(X)

Step 3: Generate the Squareform
squareform(Y)

Step 4: Find the Pairwise Distance
Y = pdist(X,'cosine')

Step 5: Find the Cluster Linkage
Z = linkage(Y,'centroid')

Step 6: Determine cophenetic correlation coefficient
c = cophenet(Z,Y)

Step 7: Construct the Dendrogram
dendrogram(Z)

Output:
c = 0.7819

5.29 Method-29: Correlation and single

Step 1: Score Matrix is generated

Step 2: Find the Distance Information
Y = pdist(X)

Step 3: Generate the Squareform
squareform(Y)

Step 4: Find the Pairwise Distance
Y = pdist(X,'correlation')

Step 5: Find the Cluster Linkage
Z = linkage(Y,'single')

Step 6: Determine cophenetic correlation coefficient
c = cophenet(Z,Y)

Step 7: Construct the Dendrogram
dendrogram(Z)

Output:
c = NaN

5.30 Method-30: Correlation and complete

Step 1: Score Matrix is generated

Step 2: Find the Distance Information
Y = pdist(X)

Step 3: Generate the Squareform
squareform(Y)

Step 4: Find the Pairwise Distance
Y = pdist(X,'correlation')

Step 5: Find the Cluster Linkage
Z = linkage(Y,'complete')

Step 6: Determine cophenetic correlation coefficient
c = cophenet(Z,Y)

Step 7: Construct the Dendrogram
dendrogram(Z)

Output:
c = NaN

5.31 Method-31: Correlation and average

Step 1: Score Matrix is generated

Step 2: Find the Distance Information
Y = pdist(X)

Step 3: Generate the Squareform
squareform(Y)

Step 4: Find the Pairwise Distance
Y = pdist(X,'correlation')

Step 5: Find the Cluster Linkage
Z = linkage(Y,'average')

Step 6: Determine cophenetic correlation coefficient
c = cophenet(Z,Y)

Step 7: Construct the Dendrogram
dendrogram(Z)

Output:
c = Nan

5.32 Method-32: Correlation and centroid

Step 1: Score Matrix is generated

Step 2: Find the Distance Information
Y = pdist(X)

Step 3: Generate the Squareform
squareform(Y)

Step 4: Find the Pairwise Distance
Y = pdist(X,'correlation')

Step 5: Find the Cluster Linkage
Z = linkage(Y,'centroid')

Step 6: Determine cophenetic correlation coefficient
c = cophenet(Z,Y)

Step 7: Construct the Dendrogram
dendrogram(Z)

Output:
c = NaN

5.33 Method-33: Spearman and single

Step 1: Score Matrix is generated

Step 2: Find the Distance Information
Y = pdist(X)

Step 3: Generate the Squareform
squareform(Y)

Step 4: Find the Pairwise Distance
Y = pdist(X,'spearman')

Step 5: Find the Cluster Linkage
Z = linkage(Y,'single')

Step 6: Determine cophenetic correlation coefficient
c = cophenet(Z,Y)

Step 7: Construct the Dendrogram
dendrogram(Z)

Output:
c = NaN

5.34 Method-34: Spearman and complete

Step 1: Score Matrix is generated

Step 2: Find the Distance Information
Y = pdist(X)

Step 3: Generate the Squareform
squareform(Y)

Step 4: Find the Pairwise Distance
Y = pdist(X,'spearman')

Step 5: Find the Cluster Linkage
Z = linkage(Y,'complete')

Step 6: Determine cophenetic correlation coefficient
c = cophenet(Z,Y)

Step 7: Construct the Dendrogram
dendrogram(Z)

Output:
c = NaN

5.35 Method-35: Spearman and average

Step 1: Score Matrix is generated

Step 2: Find the Distance Information
Y = pdist(X)

Step 3: Generate the Squareform
squareform(Y)

Step 4: Find the Pairwise Distance
Y = pdist(X,'spearman')

Step 5: Find the Cluster Linkage
Z = linkage(Y,'average')

Step 6: Determine cophenetic correlation coefficient
c = cophenet(Z,Y)

Step 7: Construct the Dendrogram
dendrogram(Z)

Output:
c = NaN

5.36 Method-36: Spearman and centroid

Step 1: Score Matrix is generated

Step 2: Find the Distance Information
Y = pdist(X)

Step 3: Generate the Squareform
squareform(Y)

Step 4: Find the Pairwise Distance
Y = pdist(X,'spearman')

Step 5: Find the Cluster Linkage
Z = linkage(Y,'centroid')

Step 6: Determine cophenetic correlation coefficient
c = cophenet(Z,Y)

Step 7: Construct the Dendrogram
dendrogram(Z)

Output:
c = NaN

5.37 Method-37: Hamming and single

Step 1: Score Matrix is generated

Step 2: Find the Distance Information
Y = pdist(X)

Step 3: Generate the Squareform
squareform(Y)

Step 4: Find the Pairwise Distance
Y = pdist(X,'hamming')

Step 5: Find the Cluster Linkage
Z = linkage(Y,'single')

Step 6: Determine cophenetic correlation coefficient
c = cophenet(Z,Y)

Step 7: Construct the Dendrogram
dendrogram(Z)

Output:
c = 0.7836

5.38 Method-38: Hamming and complete

Step 1: Score Matrix is generated

Step 2: Find the Distance Information
Y = pdist(X)

Step 3: Generate the Squareform
squareform(Y)

Step 4: Find the Pairwise Distance
Y = pdist(X,'hamming')

Step 5: Find the Cluster Linkage
Z = linkage(Y,'complete')

Step 6: Determine cophenetic correlation coefficient
c = cophenet(Z,Y)

Step 7: Construct the Dendrogram
dendrogram(Z)

Output:
c = 0.9036

5.39 Method-39: Hamming and average

Step 1: Score Matrix is generated

Step 2: Find the Distance Information
Y = pdist(X)

Step 3: Generate the Squareform
squareform(Y)

Step 4: Find the Pairwise Distance
Y = pdist(X,'hamming')

Step 5: Find the Cluster Linkage
Z = linkage(Y,'average')

Step 6: Determine cophenetic correlation coefficient
c = cophenet(Z,Y)

Step 7: Construct the Dendrogram
dendrogram(Z)

Output:
c = 0.9168

5.40 Method-40: Hamming and centroid

Step 1: Score Matrix is generated

Step 2: Find the Distance Information
Y = pdist(X)

Step 3: Generate the Squareform
squareform(Y)

Step 4: Find the Pairwise Distance
Y = pdist(X,'hamming')

Step 5: Find the Cluster Linkage
Z = linkage(Y,'centroid')

Step 6: Determine cophenetic correlation coefficient
c = cophenet(Z,Y)

Step 7: Construct the Dendrogram
dendrogram(Z)

Output:
c = 0.9122

5.41 Method-41: Jaccard and single

Step 1: Score Matrix is generated

Step 2: Find the Distance Information
Y = pdist(X)

Step 3: Generate the Squareform
squareform(Y)

Step 4: Find the Pairwise Distance
Y = pdist(X,'jaccard')

Step 5: Find the Cluster Linkage
Z = linkage(Y,'single')

Step 6: Determine cophenetic correlation coefficient
c = cophenet(Z,Y)

Step 7: Construct the Dendrogram
dendrogram(Z)

Output:
c = 0.7836

5.42 Method-42: Jaccard and complete

Step 1: Score Matrix is generated

Step 2: Find the Distance Information
Y = pdist(X)

Step 3: Generate the Squareform
squareform(Y)

Step 4: Find the Pairwise Distance
Y = pdist(X,'jaccard')

Step 5: Find the Cluster Linkage
Z = linkage(Y,'complete')

Step 6: Determine cophenetic correlation coefficient
c = cophenet(Z,Y)

Step 7: Construct the Dendrogram
dendrogram(Z)

Output:
c = 0.9036

5.43 Method-43: Jaccard and average

Step 1: Score Matrix is generated

Step 2: Find the Distance Information
Y = pdist(X)

Step 3: Generate the Squareform
squareform(Y)

Step 4: Find the Pairwise Distance
Y = pdist(X,'jaccard')

Step 5: Find the Cluster Linkage
Z = linkage(Y,'average')

Step 6: Determine cophenetic correlation coefficient
c = cophenet(Z,Y)

Step 7: Construct the Dendrogram
dendrogram(Z)

Output:
c = 0.9168

5.44 Method-44: Jaccard and centroid

Step 1: Score Matrix is generated

Step 2: Find the Distance Information
Y = pdist(X)

Step 3: Generate the Squareform
squareform(Y)

Step 4: Find the Pairwise Distance
Y = pdist(X,'jaccard')

Step 5: Find the Cluster Linkage
Z = linkage(Y,'centroid')

Step 6: Determine cophenetic correlation coefficient
c = cophenet(Z,Y)

Step 7: Construct the Dendrogram
dendrogram(Z)

Output:
c = 0.9122

www.ingramcontent.com/pod-product-compliance
Lightning Source LLC
Chambersburg PA
CBHW030935180526
45163CB00002B/580